A LINCOLN TREASURE TROVE

A
LINCOLN
TREASURE
TROVE

SECOND EDITION

FRED ANTIL, ED.D.

TABLE OF CONTENTS

ACKNOWLEDGMENTS

I never met my hero Abraham Lincoln (but I did shake hands with a man who had shaken hands with a woman who had shaken hands with Lincoln. Does that count?)

Nevertheless, I am fortunate to know another great man, one who is indirectly responsible for my getting into this whole Lincoln business. Without his involvement in getting me to leave New York City for upstate New York I am confident I would never have gotten into History and Lincoln as I did.

Charles F. "Chuck" Feeney has revolutionized philanthropy. His "Giving While Living" philosophy, and decision to give away his eight-billion-dollar fortune during his lifetime, has motivated many of the world's wealthiest individuals to sign a pact to do the same.

Chuck and I were contemporary undergraduates at Cornell; we all knew Chuck as the Sandwich Man. An Air Force veteran, he put himself through school on the G.I. Bill, and by selling sandwiches door to door in the dorms and fraternities. We were both enrolled in the university's renowned School of Hotel Administration (now part of SC Johnson School of Business).

Our careers took different paths but we remained in touch. His "Duty Free Shops" made him extremely wealthy, a story wonderfully told in the book, *The Billionaire Who Wasn't*, by Conor O'Clery (so titled because while Chuck was listed on all the Billionaire lists in the 1980s he had already turned over his stock to his Atlantic Philanthropies Foundation. So, while it was worth billions, he wasn't).

When called by O'Clery, asking to interview me for the book he was writing about Chuck, I replied that his friends didn't talk about him. He assured me that this was an authorized biography. After verifying this I shared some stories for the book.

One of those anecdotes had to do with an exchange of notes between us. Chuck had decided to sell his company and the press began to write about how this "anonymous philanthropist" had been secretly giving away billions of dollars over the years. They wrote stories describing some of his major contributions. I dropped Chuck a note joking that the press had it all wrong. I said that his having approached me with an attractive offer to return to Cornell as a special assistant to Jack Clark, the dynamic new dean of the hotel school, topped all his other acts. Jack became a good friend as did his wife Pat. It was Pat who introduced me, a divorced man, to her best friend Ann, a widow with six, mostly grown, children. We married and thus meeting her was, as I explained to Chuck, certainly his most important contribution to mankind.

Going along with my lame humor, and always the businessman, he wrote, "I am pleased for you, but I don't think you read the small print, 'Matrimonial Introductions, 10% of lifetime earnings. P.S. if it doesn't work out, 10% rebate.'"

One of Ann's grandchildren, Carolyn, was the first of my many grandchildren to invite me to speak to her class. Without Chuck's fortuitous intervention in my life, my Lincoln "career" would probably have never happened. Thanks Chuck (and thanks, Carolyn!).

Thanks too, to my two extended, and extensive, families. To Ann, Jane; Torie, Abigail, James I.; Fred "Bif" Jr.; Michelle, Chris, Andrew L., Nick; Cathy N., Bob, David, Anna, Dan, Lindsey, Mallory, Meredith, Paul, Amy, Finn, Rose; Marie, Jim M., Carolyn, Julia, Steve; Tom C., Janice, Brian, Catherine C., Natalie, Sam, Leo; Jim C., Elaine, Andrew C., Jackie, Peter, Charles; Rob; Joanne, Jake, Matt, Grace. They helped me make Lincoln come alive.

Finally, thanks to fellow Ann's Choice residents, Bob and Bernice Chast, for introducing me to their daughter, Linda Franklin, a gifted editor and wordsmith. Her assistance was invaluable, and I am grateful that she introduced me to the talented team at Inkwater Press.

ONE MAN'S SEARCH FOR ABRAHAM LINCOLN

" **...and** *so did Abraham Lincoln."* Thus ended a long forgotten speech delivered by a nervous high school student in an oratorical contest decades ago. It not only helped me win the contest – it indicated my early interest in Lincoln.

Many years later, some 25 years ago, I was invited by a granddaughter to read to her class on grandparents' day. My Lincoln interest kicked in and I brought Lincoln books to read to the children. Soon other grandchildren began making the same request. After a few such readings I figured that since I was about Lincoln's size, and about as handsome, why not dress up like him and try to make it a little more real for the children. A costume shop provided the top hat, vest, long black coat, bow tie, and fake beard.

It wasn't long before I began to get invitations from adult audiences. I knew that while my makeshift costume and limited Lincoln knowledge might work with the children, both had to change dramatically if I were to properly serve adult audiences. I got an authentic period suit and hat. I also grow, and darken, my own beard when asked to perform. To finalize my transformation I add a prominent mole (the tip of an eraser) to my right cheek. Once, in a fourth grade class, an excited young girl looked up and asked, "Can I touch your mole?" Knowing it was my last event that day I replied, "You can do better than that, you can have it." I pulled it off and handed it to her. She was startled but took it. Later, when the class sent a thank you note she signed it, "Your friend, the mole girl."

More important than the physical transformation, my study of Lincoln began in earnest. I've accumulated an extensive Lincoln library, collecting and reading everything possible about this remarkable man. I also have visited every place that Lincoln lived or spent much time, and many Civil War battle sites. Traveling light, but never without my journal in which I take notes, I've visited his two homes in Kentucky; the farm in Indiana where he spent his teen years; New Salem, Illinois, where he spent his twenties; and Springfield, Illinois, where he spent much of his adult life. Visiting his home, his third law office, the Legislative building in which he served, the Depot where he gave his farewell on his departure for DC, the family burial site, and, of course, the wonderful Lincoln Museum, make Springfield a Lincoln treasure trove. But no study of Lincoln would be complete without a visit to Washington, DC. The White House; the Soldiers' Home, where the family spent summers; Ford's Theatre, where he was shot; and the Petersen Boarding House, where he died – all are moving and memorable. Also unforgettable is the Lincoln Memorial, a fitting tribute to an outstanding man.

While my focus was on Lincoln I also try to learn as much about the Civil War as possible. Visits to Fort Sumter, South Carolina, where it started, and to Appomattox, Virginia, where it essentially ended, and many of the major battlefields in between – Manassas, Chancellorsville, Fredericksburg, Petersburg, Atlanta, Richmond, Antietam, Shiloh, Gettysburg, Vicksburg, Fort Donelson, New Orleans, and Nashville – provided graphic reminders of the bloody and terrible price paid to preserve the Union.

I tailor each talk to the audience I will be addressing so am constantly researching different aspects of Lincoln history to meet the interest of each particular audience.

At one Lincoln Day dinner in upstate New York I was to introduce the main speaker, New York City Mayor Rudy Giuliani. I said, "Mr. Mayor, you represent one of my favorite cities. My hero, George Washington, was sworn into office and gave his farewell address there. That makes your city special for me, but in addition I once gave a speech there that some say won me the election. Tell me, sir, is the Cooper Institute still there?" Looking up at me he bellowed, "Mr.

President, it is not only still there but I was there last week and they still talk about your speech!"

When invited to introduce the main speaker at a major Cornell University event I was asked, "You only have five minutes, is that sufficient?" I replied, "I gave the Gettysburg Address in under three minutes, I can do wonders in five minutes."

One of my most moving moments as Lincoln came after a presentation to a class in Andover, Massachusetts. I wrap up each session with children by telling them the history of the Lincoln penny – first minted in 1909, the centennial celebration of his birth, and the first American coin with an image of a real person on its face. I then distribute a penny to each student as my "calling card." The day after this presentation I got a call from the teacher telling me of a tearful call she had received from a student's mother. It seems her daughter suffered from what is called Selective Mutism; though she could speak, she chose not to. That afternoon this young girl went home clutching her penny, and wouldn't stop talking about meeting Mr. Lincoln. Her mother was ecstatic.

After giving many hundreds of Lincoln presentations I only can say that the more I learn about Abraham Lincoln the more I realize how lucky this country was to have had him as its leader. Because, as his Secretary of War, Edwin Stanton, reportedly said, "Now he belongs to the ages."

Fred Antil, EdD.

MY RENDEZVOUS WITH HISTORY

I admittedly came to my passion for History rather late in life. As mentioned in the "One Man's Search for Lincoln" section, I started researching Lincoln as I was nearing retirement, a quarter of a century ago. But it was moving from upstate New York to the suburbs of Philadelphia that broadened my historical perspective. Here the interest in the Colonial and Revolutionary War era is as great as is the interest in the Civil War. I have joined several Civil War Roundtable groups, and serve on the Boards of Craven Hall (a restored Colonial farmhouse), and the John Fitch Museum (inventor of the steamboat).

Those of us interested in History live in a marvelous time. Thanks to technology we have the resources of the Library of Congress, the Smithsonian, and other varied sources available to us via the Internet. I live in a vibrant 2,000-plus-resident retirement community, and have been able to restart a monthly

History Club program because of the wealth of visual and other material from the Web. While knowing a great deal about Lincoln I am now able to lead an informative and interesting program on almost any historical topic. [See programs below.] Over a year ago we started in a 50-seat classroom but quickly outgrew our space. We now meet in the 250-seat auditorium.

HISTORY CLUB - PAST PROGRAMS

PEOPLE

Lincoln (Movie), the 13th Amendment (part 1)

Lincoln (Movie), the 13th amendment (part 2)

Ben Franklin

Lincoln, the Man not the Myth

Unknown people who made a difference

Remarkable Women, Founding Mothers

Mark Twain

Theodore Roosevelt

Alexander Hamilton

Black musical legends (90th birthday of MLK Jr.)

Mary Todd, and other women in Lincoln's life

An Eyewitness to History – The Warsaw Ghetto

The "Unsinkable " Titanic

Daniel Boone, Davy Crockett, Kit Carson and Wild Bill Hickok

Remarkable Women – Four Civil War Generals' Wives

Lincoln and the Silver Screen

The Greatest Showman, P.T. Barnum

PLACES

New Orleans – Music, Mardi Gras, 1814 Battle

Warminster, PA – History in our own backyard

Roman Britain (AD 43 – AD 410)

New Netherland and New Amsterdam

EVENTS

The Rape of Nanking, 1937

Songs of War – Civil, Cuba, WWI, WWII

World War I, Centennial of Armistice

The 9/11 Attacks, An Eyewitness to History

Country Music and America's History

Romance and Intrigue in the Palace, Abdication of a King

IDEAS

The Rational Optimist, Matt Ridley

The Making of the Constitution

History not in your American History Book

Playboy Clubs – the real story

To me History has proven to be both comforting and frustrating.

Comforting in that occasionally I am convinced we live in the absolutely craziest of times ever – politically, socially, environmentally, you name it. But then a study of History shows us there were many past periods that match or even exceed our current experiences.

Frustrating in that while it is relatively easy to find

accurate, objective, fact- based History, the "Who," "What," "When," and "Where." Assuming, of course, reliable sources, both primary and secondary. However, accurate, subjective aspects of History – the "How" and the "Why" – prove much more challenging. Understanding the context and the setting of the time in which the "facts" occurred is essential, but these areas can be distorted by bias and personal feelings of the source and/or the historian.

It is of this aspect of History that Mark Twain wrote, "The very ink with which history is written is merely fluid prejudice." We need not be as cynical as Mr. Twain to understand the need to study a number of versions of the same historical event to truly begin to "know" it.

For instance, most of us now accept Lincoln as a great American leader, an icon. But there are a number of books highly critical of him as a man, and as a leader. I once asked a young professor at a prestigious university what surprised him most about the students he saw in his American History class. He said he was surprised at how many of his young students came with a preconceived negative opinion of Lincoln.

Both sides of the argument use "research" and "facts" to justify their stands, but both sides can't be right. To understand History, one must study many different reports about any given person, place, event, or issue, and ultimately make one's own decision about which are more accurate.

I

LINCOLN LORE - LESSER-KNOWN STORIES ABOUT ABRAHAM LINCOLN

THE BIRTHPLACE OF PRESIDENTS

There have been 44 men, born in 21 different states, who have served as president. [Yes, I know we have had 45 presidents, so how come just 44 different men? One man, Grover Cleveland, was elected two separate, not consecutive, times.]

Over half of them came from four states: Virginia – eight; Ohio – seven; New York – five; Massachusetts – four. But only one state, Kentucky, has produced two American presidents who served at the same time – the first president(s) born outside the original thirteen colonies.

Abraham Lincoln, the president of the USA, and Jefferson Davis, who would become the president of the CSA

1

(Confederate States of America), were born one year and one hundred miles apart in Kentucky. Davis actually became president before Lincoln. He was sworn in as president of the Confederacy on February 18, 1861. Lincoln was sworn in as president of the USA on March 4, 1861.

Besides being born in the same state their lives intertwined in interesting ways over the years.

They both served in the military at the same time. Davis was a West Point graduate, while Lincoln served a month as a Captain (elected by his fellow troops) and then a month as a private in the Illinois militia. Lincoln was involved in the Black Hawk War, but saw no action. Lieutenant Davis was assigned to take the Indian chief Black Hawk to prison after he was captured (Black Hawk later reported that Davis treated him with great kindness). More than a decade later Lincoln and Davis served at the same time in Congress for a couple of years, Lincoln in the House of Representatives, and Davis in the Senate.

After Lincoln was elected president, his wife, Mary, hired and became very good friends with Elizabeth Keckley, an outstanding seamstress and former slave. Ms. Keckley had earlier done work for Jefferson Davis's wife when he was in Washington.

Both presidents also shared a presidential tragedy: eleven-year-old Willie Lincoln died of illness in the White House; and Jefferson Davis's five-year-old son Joseph Davis died from falling off the roof of the Confederate White House in Richmond.

After the fall of Richmond Lincoln and his son Tad walked through the streets of Richmond, and Lincoln sat in Davis's chair in the Confederate White House.

OH! WHY SHOULD THE SPIRIT OF MORTAL BE PROUD?

Lincoln knew death; some would say he was fascinated by it. But he was fatalistic, and careless about his own safety. During his young adulthood some friends actually felt that he, on at least two occasions, was suicidal. As an adult one of his favorite poems, one he could recite from memory, was *Mortality* by William Knox. It talks about the inevitability of death.

MORTALITY

(two of fourteen verses)

Oh! why should the spirit of mortal be proud?
Like a swift-fleeting meteor, a fast-flying cloud
A flash of the lightning, a break of the wave
He passeth from life to his rest in the grave.

'Tis the wink of an eye – 'tis the draught of a breath –
From the blossom of health to the paleness of death,
From the gilded saloon to the bier and the shroud: –
Oh! why should the spirit of mortal be proud?

He had lost his mother when he was nine. When he was nineteen, his twenty-one-year-old sister, Sarah, died in childbirth. A dear friend, some say a sweetheart, Ann Rutledge, died at twenty-three. Lincoln had four sons, two of whom died before him.

As a young boy he once shot a wild turkey. It bothered him so much that he never hunted again. Ironically, this man who could not kill an animal presided over one of the bloodiest wars in history, a war that quickly touched him personally. The first Union officer killed was a very close family friend, Col. Elmer Ellsworth. Ellsworth had clerked in Lincoln's Springfield law office and had come to Washington with Lincoln. A month or so after the war had actually started Ellsworth was stationed at the White House and because Lincoln and others had expressed frustration at seeing a Confederate flag flying across the Potomac in

Alexandria, Virginia, Ellsworth led a small military contingent to the small hotel where it was flying and removed it. The proprietor shot and killed Ellsworth. Lincoln was devastated and Ellsworth received a formal state funeral at the White House. A few months after this, a long-time professional and personal friend of Lincoln's, Edward Baker, was killed at the Battle of Ball's Bluff, Virginia. Lincoln had even named his second son after this man.

Civil War deaths were not limited to his friends. Mary Todd Lincoln was raised in Lexington, Kentucky, in a slave-holding family. Mary was the fourth child in a family of seven when her mother died and her father remarried. There were nine children in his second marriage, all half-brothers or half-sisters to Mary. Kentucky did not secede from the Union, but many, including the Todd family, sympathized with the Southern cause. One brother, three half-brothers, and one brother-in-law fought for the Confederacy. Two half-brothers were killed, one wounded, and her brother-in-law, a Confederate general, was killed. Both Abraham and Mary Lincoln knew the sorrow of war.

Lincoln himself escaped death a number of times. As a young boy in Kentucky he was saved from drowning by a slightly older childhood friend. At 10, in Indiana, he was kicked in the head by a horse and was thought to be dead for a time, until finally recovering. During his presidency his family would avoid the DC heat by spending the summer at a cottage near the Soldiers' Home a few miles from the White House. While he was riding home from his White House office one night a shot went through his hat. After that he was accompanied by a military guard, but he remained cavalier about his own safety. One Confederate raid reached the Maryland and DC border. Lincoln went to the federal barricades to see for himself what was happening. At one point a Union officer, not recognizing who it was, yelled, "Get down you damn fool, you will get shot." After the Confederate leadership fled their capital, Richmond, he and his 10-year-old son walked through the city with a very small protective force.

Lincoln's visit to Indiana in 1846 inspired this poem:

MY CHILDHOOD HOME I SEE AGAIN
(three of ten verses)

My childhood's home I see again,
And sadden with the view;
And still, as memory crowds my brain,
There's pleasure in it too.

I hear the loved survivors tell
How nought from death could save,
Till every sound appears a knell,
And every spot a grave.

I range the fields with pensive tread,
And pace the hollow rooms,
And feel (companion of the dead)
I'm living in the tombs.

Lincoln movingly expressed his own feelings about death

in the following letter of condolence he wrote to the daughter of his long-time friend, William McCullough. Back when Lincoln was on the law circuit, McCullough was sheriff as well as clerk of the McLean County Circuit Court in Bloomington, Illinois. McCullough helped organize the Fourth Illinois Cavalry early in the Civil War. On December 5, 1862, when he was serving as Lieutenant Colonel, he lost his life during a night charge near Coffeeville, Mississippi.

In his letter Lincoln seemed to be remembering his own childhood grief in 1818 following his mother's death after a short illness. And much more recent and more painful was the death on February 20, 1862, of his beloved 11-year-old son Willie.

Executive Mansion,
Washington, December 23, 1862.

Dear Fanny

It is with deep grief that I learn of the death of your kind and brave Father; and, especially, that it is affecting your young heart beyond what is common in such cases. In this sad world of ours, sorrow comes to all; and, to the young, it comes with bitterest agony, because it takes them unawares. The older have learned to ever expect it. I am anxious to afford some alleviation of your present distress. Perfect relief is not possible, except with time. You can not now realize that you will ever feel better. Is not this so? And yet it is a mistake.

You are sure to be happy again. To know this, which is certainly true, will make you some less miserable now. I have had experience enough to know what I say; and you need only to believe it, to feel better at once. The memory of your dear Father, instead of an agony, will yet be a sad sweet feeling in your heart, of a purer and holier sort than you have known before.

Please present my kind regards to your afflicted mother.

Your sincere friend
A. Lincoln

Lincoln's attitude toward death is best understood when one examines his complicated approach to faith and religious beliefs. It might be said that Lincoln was a spiritual man, not necessarily a religious one.

His youthful questioning of certain aspects of organized religion caused him political problems later in life. They tell of him attending a "fire and brimstone" revival meeting where at some point the preacher asked the attendees who intended to go to heaven to rise. Then he called on those who wished to go to hell to stand. He then said, "Mr. Lincoln, you have not expressed an interest in going to either heaven or hell. May I enquire as to where you do plan to go?" Lincoln replied, "I did not come with the idea of being singled out, but since you ask, I will reply with equal candor, I intend to go to Congress."

At the age of 46 he felt it necessary to declare, "That I am not a member of any Christian Church is true, but I have never denied the truth of the Scriptures; and I have never spoken with intentional disrespect of religion in general, or of any denomination of Christians in particular."

He was introduced to the Bible early in his life. It helped him learn to read and write, and he quoted from it frequently. In 1864 he was presented with a Bible by the Loyal Colored People of Baltimore and he remarked, "In regard to this Great book, I have but to say it is the best gift God has given to man." Historians say there were six Abraham Lincoln family Bibles. The latest resurfaced 150 years after his death, and is now in the Lincoln Museum in Springfield.

[Another Bible owned by Lincoln was used by former President Barack Obama at his 2009 and 2013 inaugurations, and it was also used by President Trump at his 2017 inauguration.]

Lincoln certainly became more publicly connected with God as he grew older. During his presidency he frequently wrote or spoke about God's role in our destiny. His second Inaugural Address, a month before his death, was a moving sermon, worthy of any church pulpit (see page 196).

TEENAGER LINCOLN, ESQ.

Lincoln officially became a lawyer when he was 27 after years of self-study and having satisfied a judge that he knew enough law to be licensed to practice. In fact he actually won his first law case when he was 15. At one point in his youthful efforts to earn money, he used his homemade skiff to row passengers to the middle of the Ohio River to board the steamboat. He was sued by the ferryboat operator who had the franchise to transport people from the Indiana side of the river to the Kentucky side, and back. Lincoln told the judge that he was not taking people across the river, just to the middle. The judge agreed and threw out the case. Lincoln grew up to become one of the most successful lawyers in Illinois. No one ever argued more cases before the Illinois Supreme Court than he did.

ATTORNEY AT LAW SUI GENERIS! (IN A CLASS BY HIMSELF) *

L incoln's instinctive intellectual curiosity had led him to know something about the law long before he decided to

---

* In February 2020, the editor of the *CBA Record*, the Chicago Bar Association's journal, honored Lincoln's birthday in its "Editor's Briefcase" column, *10 Intriguing Facts about Abraham Lincoln*. Credit for the information was given to this book, *A Lincoln Treasure Trove* (first edition). I was honored that even in a small way I could be a part of Chicago and Illinois recognizing and celebrating one of its most renowned fellow lawyers.

strive toward becoming an attorney. As a teenager in Indiana and a young man in Illinois he was constantly searching for things to read and opportunities to learn. There were few libraries, so he would go to courthouses to read statutes, laws, case reviews, etc. Being fascinated by public speaking and communications, he would also sit in on court cases when possible. In 1831 he actually wrote out his first legal document for a friend in New Salem.

In 1834 he borrowed law books from his friend John Todd Stuart, who had encouraged him to take up this new endeavor, and started to seriously pursue a law career. In 1836 he received a license to practice law in all Illinois state courts. In 1837 he moved to Springfield and became a junior partner in Stuart's law office. The next year he successfully represented his client in a murder case (*People v. Truett*). From 1834 to 1842 he served in the state legislature, so he was involved with the passage of laws as well as working with clients in his office and courtrooms.

In 1839 he started practicing law on the Illinois Eighth Judicial Circuit. This included almost 10 counties in an area 120 miles long and 85 miles wide. Lawyers on the circuit were on the road for seven or eight weeks each spring and early fall. A judge traveled with a few lawyers and they took care of the local legal business at each circuit courthouse before moving on to the next. Courthouses ranged from dignified buildings to dilapidated structures with noisy animals nearby. One small town in this area was formed during the early 1850s and ended up calling itself Lincoln, in honor of the circuit lawyer who helped them. Lincoln, Illinois, is the only town that was named for him before he became president.

Traveling the circuit was arduous, roads were rough, and many streams and creeks might or might not have bridges. Travel was on horseback or perhaps by horse and buggy. One of Lincoln's legends, that he carried his papers in his stovepipe hat, came from his having to cross small streams and, not wanting to get his saddlebags wet, would put some papers in his hat. Sleeping and eating accommodations were primitive at best. If one was lucky enough to get a bed instead of the floor, the bed usually would have at least two occupants, maybe three. When his friend, Judge David Davis, was traveling with him, the judge often was the only one who got his own bed. This was for two reasons: one, his status as the judge, and two, he was close to 300 pounds. The highlights of this circuit for Lincoln were often the evenings when the men would gather and share stories and jokes. Lincoln was frequently the star of these gatherings. Occasionally, in the absence of a judge, Lincoln would serve as the interim judge.

In 1840 he argued his first case before the Illinois Supreme Court, the first of 175 total cases.

In 1841 his partnership with Stuart ended, and Lincoln became a law partner of Stephen Logan. Logan introduced Lincoln to new areas of law, bigger courts, and bigger cases. This partnership ended in 1844 when Logan wanted his son to join the firm, and Lincoln wanted to form his own firm. William "Billy" Herndon became his junior partner, and

Lincoln and Herndon remained the name of the firm until Lincoln's death. Nobody was more surprised than Herndon that Lincoln selected him. He once said that Mr. Lincoln was the most generous, forbearing, and charitable man he ever knew.

Herndon, nine years younger than Lincoln, had been a clerk in Lincoln's friend, Joshua Speed's, store when they had met. Lincoln lived above the store until he got married. Herndon began studying the law and then clerking in Lincoln's law office. Herndon had just earned his license to practice when Lincoln invited him to be his partner. Everyone in Springfield who knew Lincoln was astounded, and Mary never really got over it. She never invited Herndon to dinner in their home. Even when he traveled to Washington to visit the new president Herndon didn't receive a family invitation. After the president's death Herndon got even and spent years spreading the story, now seriously questioned, that Lincoln's real true love was Ann Rutledge, a woman whom he knew in New Salem and who died very young. Herndon was also highly critical of Willie and Tad Lincoln. He felt their father spoiled them, which he did, and they frequently made doing work in the office almost impossible.

Lincoln's ethical core influenced his behavior in his chosen profession, the Law, and he practiced what he preached.

"Let no young man choosing the law for a calling for a moment yield to the popular belief – resolve to be honest at all events; and if in your own judgment you cannot be an honest lawyer, resolve to be honest without being a lawyer."

- Keep fees reasonable. [His fees were in the $5 to $20 range, though much higher with corporate clients. He once charged a railroad company $5,000. They balked, saying, "You are charging New York fees." He replied, "You got New York results." He received his fee, but only after suing the company.]

- Discourage litigation. Try to convince both parties that it is better for both sides to compromise and settle without going to trial.

- Determine to devote a certain amount of time to pro bono work – free legal work for those who cannot afford legal services.

- Lincoln's strength as a lawyer was his ability to simplify cases. He was able to reduce even complex cases to a few key points. He put legal disputes into simple focus and had a gift for brevity and clarity. Lincoln was good at logical oral argument and also at legal research. He had a wonderful ability to "read" juries and influence them with his persuasive arguments.

Lincoln was a "jack-of-all-trades" when it came to his law practice. Generally speaking, he would accept any case (whether civil or criminal) brought before him. Lincoln and his partners handled over 5,000 cases.

As president he appointed five Supreme Court Associate Justices: Noah H. Swayne of Ohio; Samuel F. Miller of Iowa; David Davis of Illinois (a longtime friend); Stephen J. Field of California; and Salmon P. Chase of Ohio (his former Secretary of the Treasury).

[One grisly murder trial in 1859 helped raise Abraham Lincoln's national profile. The victim was one of Lincoln's former law clerks. The accused, whom Lincoln defended, was the son of one of his prominent political supporters. So, just nine months before the national convention that would nominate him as the Republican candidate for president, he was involved in *People v. Harrison*, a high-profile murder case. Lincoln worked on this case with his former law partner, Stephen Logan.

What made this case so unusual is that the *Illinois State Journal* had hired a transcriber to take down every word. Robert Hitt would provide a daily transcript for its readers. Hitt was the same man who had transcribed the seven three-hour long Lincoln-Douglas debates, which were published and very popular. Transcriptions of actual trials were still extremely rare. The jury decided for Lincoln's client. His national reputation only continued to grow. Abraham Lincoln was on his way to fulfill his destiny as chief magistrate of the land!]

CAPTAIN LINCOLN, IT RUNS IN THE FAMILY

When the Black Hawk War broke out in 1832 the 23-year-old Lincoln joined the state militia for a one-month enlistment. At that time the troops elected their own officers. He was elected Captain and was immensely proud of that recognition. At the end of the month he re-enlisted for another month, as a private. Coincidentally the officer in charge of Fort Sumter at the beginning of the Civil War was Robert Anderson. Anderson was a Colonel in the Illinois Militia during the Black Hawk War and mustered Abraham Lincoln out of the militia after his first month of service and then again after his second. [Abraham Lincoln was given two parcels of land in Iowa because of his service in the Black Hawk War, 40 acres in 1850 and 120 acres in 1855. Lincoln owned the land until his death in 1865, when it went to his widow and two surviving sons.]

During the Civil War, Lincoln's oldest son, Robert, served on General Grant's staff – as a Captain. He was with Grant when Lee surrendered at Appomattox.

Lincoln's grandfather, Abraham Lincoln, the man for whom he was named, was a Captain in the Virginia Militia during the Revolutionary War.

[In 1786, his grandfather Abraham was killed by marauding Indians on his farm in Kentucky. President Lincoln's father, Thomas, was eight at the time. Thomas's fourteen-year-old brother, Mordecai, killed the Indian, who was reaching for young Tom.]

LINCOLN LORE #6

A DUEL, BUT NO PISTOLS!

In 1842 Lincoln mocked an Illinois politician in an anonymous letter to a newspaper. His letter was signed "Rebecca."
Mary Todd, who would marry Lincoln two months later,
thought the letter funny and so she and a girlfriend wrote an
equally mocking, anonymous letter about that politician to
the same newspaper. The man, James Shields, found out that
Lincoln had written the letter and challenged him to a duel.
Lincoln, not wanting Mary Todd's name disclosed, admitted
to being the author. He was reluctant but knew, for his legal
and political career, he could not refuse the duel challenge.
He had the choice of weapons, and knowing Shields was a
marksman, chose broadswords (Lincoln didn't know that
at one time in his life Shields actually taught fencing). At

the dueling site Lincoln used his long arms to cut leaves off overhead trees. Seeing this, the much shorter Shields decided it might be time to talk out their differences, which they did. The duel was called off. This remained one of the most embarrassing events in Lincoln's life.

Later Shields and Lincoln became friends, and during the Civil War Shields was appointed a General by Lincoln. Shields has the distinction of being the only person to serve as senator from three different states.

Lincoln was the second and last president to have been involved in a duel. It is estimated Andrew Jackson participated in between five and one hundred duels before he became president in 1829. He actually carried a bullet in his chest from a duel. He allowed the other person to fire first, and was shot. He then killed his opponent, Charles Dickinson, a fellow plantation owner who had slandered Jackson's wife.

MOVE OVER THOMAS EDISON, BUT NOT ON DUMBO

Lincoln is the only president with a patent. He was 40 when he invented a device to help stuck steamboats get off a sandbar. It was really never put into operation, but the model he submitted is in the Smithsonian.

Lincoln knew steamboats well and spent a great deal of time on rivers. As a boy he earned money by rowing people out to the middle of the Ohio River to board the steamboat. As a young man he took two trips on flatboats to New Orleans. He once piloted a boat on the Sangamon River when he lived in New Salem, Illinois. As an adult he traveled on the rivers and Great Lakes and as president he used a steamboat often to visit General Grant in the field. Coincidentally, the inventor of the steamboat, John Fitch of Warminster, Pennsylvania, died and is buried just a few miles from where Lincoln was born in Kentucky.

President Lincoln mentioned the importance of steam, both on our rivers and our land, in a reply to a letter from the King of Siam in which he politely declined the King's offer to send us elephants to be beasts of burden and for transportation.

Lincoln actually loved technology. He signed the bill to develop transcontinental train transportation, revolutionized the use of the telegraph, and pushed technical and mechanical breakthroughs during his presidency.

He also signed the Morrill Land Grant Act, which had been vetoed by his predecessor, President Buchanan. This act called for the federal government to give land to the states, which they could sell to fund new colleges of agriculture and engineering. All fifty states have at least one such Land Grant college today, with some having more than one. Land Grant schools include Cornell, MIT, Penn State, and the University of California at Berkeley.

AH, THOSE KENTUCKY BELLES

Before Lincoln proposed to, and married, Mary Todd from Lexington, Kentucky, he had proposed to a Mary Owens, also from a wealthy family in Kentucky. She had a married sister in New Salem and this woman was anxious that Mary Owens and Lincoln meet. They spent time together and Mary returned to Kentucky. At one point Lincoln half-jokingly remarked that he would marry her if she returned to Illinois. She did return but Lincoln did not really want to marry her. He wrote her several letters telling her how difficult life with him would be, but making it clear that he would go through with the marriage if she wanted it. He wasn't disappointed when she turned him down.

His uncertainty about marriage plagued his later courtship of Mary Todd too. He broke off the relationship at one point, going into a deep funk. But friends got them back together and some suggest that Mary took the lead in making the marriage happen. [Perhaps my favorite historical item is a book, *Mary Wife of Lincoln By Her Niece, Katherine Helm* (1928). It was presented to me after my Lincoln presentation to a large Women's Club. Emilie Helm, Katherine's mother, was the wife of Confederate General Benjamin Helm, and the half-sister of Mary Todd Lincoln. She and her child were in the South with her husband when he was killed in battle. Needing a military pass to get to their home in Kentucky, she appealed to her brother-in-law, Lincoln. He sent her the pass, but suggested she visit them in Washington. She did and there are a number of amusing stories about how the cousins, Katherine and Tad, both about the same age, argued about things like who was president. She insisted that Jefferson Davis was president, while he insisted that his father was. Lincoln finally settled it by saying, "I am your president, I am her Uncle Lincoln." As an adult, thanks to her unique position to research Mary's history, she wrote this fascinating book about a very complex woman.]

In general he was much more at ease with older women than he was with young ones. He boarded in many private homes and he felt more at ease sharing time with older women. In New Salem though, while, in his twenties, there was one young woman he became close to. Ann Rutledge was the daughter of the local tavern keeper and she and Lincoln became very good friends. Perhaps it was because she was engaged and therefore safe to be with as her fiancé had gone east to settle some family business and was gone for a very long time. Some say she was not only his first love, but the most important love of his life. She died very young and Lincoln was visibly heartbroken and depressed. But it is hard to determine exactly how important the actual romantic connection was. Many who spread the story did not like Mary Todd Lincoln and might have accepted as fact stories from Rutledge family members who, when talking years later about this young woman's friendship with a deceased icon, might understandably exaggerate the depth of this early relationship.

Although not from a wealthy family, Ann Rutledge, like Mary Owens and Mary Todd, was born in Kentucky.

SPRECHEN SIE DEUTSCH, HERR ABRAHAM?

braham Lincoln once owned a newspaper. Ironically, it was a German language newspaper, a language he did not read or speak. But the *Illinois Staats-Anzeiger* supported the Republican Party, and he wanted it to continue to do so through his first presidential election. The German-American vote was very important. Lincoln won the election and sold the newspaper.

LINCOLN, A WINNER OR A LOSER?

Contrary to the popular "Lincoln Failures" list, Lincoln lost only one popular vote election, his first run for the state legislature at the age of 23. Right after he had announced his candidacy, and because of the Black Hawk War, he joined the militia and couldn't campaign. He lost – the only popular vote election he ever lost. He later won four straight elections to the legislature. He ran for Congress once, and won. He ran for the presidency twice, and won both times. His name was put forth several times for important positions which he didn't get, but these were political defeats, not popular vote losses. He also ran for the Senate and got more votes than his opponent, but at that time the State Legislature chose the state's senators. There were more Democrats in that body than Republicans and they chose Stephen Douglas.

In his first presidential campaign there were four candidates. His popular vote was less than 40% of the total but he won the Electoral College. He won 55% of the vote in 1864 to earn a second term.

LINCOLN LORE #11

HIS "TEAM OF RIVALS"

Many of the men chosen by Lincoln to help run the country were political rivals and/or people who had been highly critical of him. Sometimes a Democrat (D, below) was selected for political purposes, but generally Lincoln looked for competence. One, Cameron, was appointed because of a campaign promise made by an over-eager Lincoln supporter. Ethical and incompetence issues led to Cameron's replacement by the highly competent and dedicated Stanton, a man who had at one time called Lincoln a "gorilla." Stanton had been hired to defend a client in Ohio, but because he needed a regional lawyer, Lincoln was hired. The polished Stanton was appalled by the very unpolished Lincoln and didn't use him in court. Later Lincoln returned his payment saying he didn't earn it. Stanton, Chase, and Seward were just some of his cabinet members who were sure they were more qualified to be president than the man who appointed them. They grew to respect, and at least in Seward and Stanton's case, to really admire him.

Lincoln called his Secretary of War and his Secretary of the Navy "Mars" and "Neptune" – the ancient gods of War and the Sea.

LINCOLN'S CABINET

- Vice Presidents – Hannibal Hamlin; Andrew Johnson (D) (1865)

- Secretary of State – William Seward

- Secretary of the Treasury – Salmon Chase; William Fessendon (1864); Hugh McCulloch (1865)

- Secretary of War – Simon Cameron (D then R); Edwin M. Stanton (1862)

- Attorney General – Edward Bates; James Speed (D) (1864)

- Postmaster General – Montgomery Blair; William Dennison (1864)

- Secretary of Navy – Gideon Welles

- Secretary of the Interior – Caleb B. Smith; John P. Usher (1863)

[Soon after Lincoln's death Secretary of the Interior Usher

stepped down and James Harlan was appointed by President Johnson. Harlan's daughter Mary married Robert Lincoln in 1868.]

"NOT BY THE HAIR OF MY CHINNY-CHIN-CHIN"

For the first 51 of Lincoln's 56 years on earth he did not have a beard. Lincoln, the first American president with a beard, was elected in November 1860 without one. But by the time he left for Washington in early February, to be sworn in as president in March, he had grown a beard. We will never really know his reasons, but letters between an 11-year-old girl, who suggested a beard, and Lincoln, exist. Grace Bedell wrote from Westfield, New York, that since his face was so thin a beard might help get the ladies to urge their husbands to vote for him. He responded that since he had never worn a beard, wouldn't people say it was a "piece of silly affect[a]ion" if he did? On his long trip to Washington his train stopped in Westfield, and he, with his brand-new beard, shook hands with Grace. A statue commemorating that meeting stands in the Westfield public square today.

WILLIAM H. JOHNSON, BARBER, VALET, AND FRIEND

William Johnson, a barber, was the only black person in the Lincoln entourage, which left Springfield for Washington in 1861. Lincoln hoped to have him work in the White House but Johnson was not accepted by other staff members, so Lincoln got him another government job. Johnson would visit the Executive Mansion to trim Lincoln's hair and keep him abreast of what was happening in the city. He accompanied Lincoln to Gettysburg but got sick coming back and died. Lincoln paid for his funeral and arranged for him to be buried at Arlington. He also managed to clear up some final debts Johnson had.

COMMANDER-IN-CHIEF, LITERALLY

Lincoln is the only president who visited the front lines of a war during his presidency, several times actually. At one point he even organized and led a military campaign. When on a steamboat on the Chesapeake he wondered why the federal troops were not doing anything about our major port, Norfolk, Virginia, then in the hands of the Rebels. He studied the shoreline and suggested where a landing could be made and ordered a military unit into action. It worked out well because the Confederates had figured out that they were in a precarious position and had already quietly pulled out. His one and only military campaign was a success.

36

Battle of Antietam, Maryland [Pinkerton, Lincoln, & McClernand]. Courtesy of Library of Congress.

A STATE THAT SECEDED, WITH LINCOLN'S BLESSING!

When Lincoln was elected president there were 33 states; before he was sworn in, Kansas became part of the Union, number 34.

Almost immediately, because of Lincoln's stance on slavery, seven southern states seceded from the Union (South Carolina, Mississippi, Florida, Alabama, Georgia, Louisiana, and Texas), forming the CSA (Confederate States of America). After Fort Sumter was fired on, four more states joined them (Virginia, North Carolina, Tennessee, and Arkansas). All 11 seceding states were slave-holding states.

Four other slave-holding states, Delaware, Maryland, Kentucky, and Missouri, the so-called border states, did not join the Confederacy.

The slave-holding class tended to control the politics in the southern states. But, while these states voted for secession, many of the small non-slave-holding farmers, especially in the western hill counties of the Carolinas and Virginia, preferred to stay in the Union. Agitation in Virginia from western counties for separation began almost immediately after its secession from the U.S. In 1863 West Virginia voted to "secede" from Virginia, officially becoming the 35th state in the Union. It became the fifth border state. This was the first state to secede from another since Maine had seceded from Massachusetts in 1820.

Nevada also joined the Union during Lincoln's administration. Lincoln was working hard in Washington to get Congress to pass the 13th Amendment, which would end slavery forever. He knew that getting it passed was one thing, but that it might be difficult to get it ratified by the three fourths of states that had to approve it (27 of the 36). He was especially concerned about the former slave-holding states after the war. He knew the Nevada territory was seeking statehood and also thought it would be Republican, i.e., non-pro-slavery, so he successfully encouraged its admission as the 36th state in 1864.

The Amendment became law when it was ratified in December 1865 after Georgia became the 27th state to ratify it. Lincoln had fought hard to get it passed, but he didn't live to see it ratified. How different the Reconstruction era might have been if he had lived.

Lincoln was justified in being concerned about its ratification. While it was ratified in 1865, some of the remaining nine states were slow in signing the new document. Three didn't ratify the 13th Amendment until 1901, 1976, and 1995, respectively.

[Earlier in his political career Lincoln had the opportunity to be part of the birth of another state, or perhaps states. In 1849, after completing his term in Congress, Lincoln was offered a position as Secretary of the Oregon Territory. While sparsely populated, this was an extensive area – all of what is now Oregon, Washington, Idaho, and parts of Wyoming and Montana. When he turned it down he was offered the job of Governor, which he also rejected. He really didn't want to leave Illinois politics, and returned to Springfield and his private law practice.]

DR. ABRAHAM LINCOLN, THE IVY LEAGUER

Lincoln had less than one year of formal schooling. Filling out a background form on taking his seat in Congress, after *Education*, he wrote "Defective." Nevertheless, Lincoln was awarded three honorary degrees in his lifetime. Knox College gave him a Doctor of Laws in 1860. And two institutions, later members of the Ivy League, also awarded him honorary doctorates: Columbia University (then known as King's College) an LLD in 1861, and Princeton University (then known as the College of New Jersey) an LLD in 1864.

Lincoln's letter to King's College (Columbia University) written by his secretary, John Hay, but signed by Lincoln, was written to its president, Charles King, on June 26, 1861, thanking the college for awarding him an honorary degree. Lincoln interpreted the award of this degree as a symbol of support and thanked the president of Columbia for the "manifestation of confidence and good will."

Thus, one Ivy League degree was bestowed after Lincoln's first election as the Civil War heated up, and one Ivy League degree was bestowed after Lincoln's second election, when the Civil War was winding down (Savannah had been captured). Lincoln seemed to interpret each politically.

Lincoln accepted the honorary degree of Doctor of Laws from the College of New Jersey (Princeton) in 1864 shortly after his reelection to a second term. The degree was conferred at a meeting of the trustees on December 20th of that year, and the College's president John Maclean wrote to Lincoln the same day to inform him of their action. The reply, in Lincoln's own handwriting, is one of Princeton's treasured possessions – "among the title deeds to our Americanism," as Dean Gauss once put it. The letter is as follows:

> Executive Mansion
> Washington, December 27, 1864
>
> My Dear Sir:
>
> I have the honour to acknowledge the reception of your note of the 20th of December, conveying the announcement that the Trustees of the College of New Jersey have conferred upon me the Degree of Doctor of Laws.

The assurance conveyed by this high compliment, that the course of the government which I represent has received the approval of a body of gentlemen of such character and intelligence in this time of public trial, is most grateful to me.

Thoughtful men must feel that the fate of civilization upon this continent is involved in the issue of our contest. Among the most gratifying proofs of this conviction is the hearty devotion everywhere exhibited by our schools and colleges to the national cause.

I am most thankful if my labors have seemed to conduce to the preservation of those institutions under which alone we can expect good government and in its train sound learning and the progress of the liberal arts.

I am, sir, very truly

Your obedient servant

A. LINCOLN

Dr. John Maclean

As regards to honorary degrees, this was common practice with celebrated personages. For instance Harvard and Yale awarded such degrees to George Washington, Thomas Jefferson, Benjamin Franklin, and others. Franklin, a brilliant, worldwide acclaimed scientist, was also awarded an honorary degree from Oxford. He was the only one who used the title. For the rest of his life he was known as Doctor Franklin.

Lincoln also has a close connection to another Ivy League school. Hanging on the back wall of the Tompkins County Public Library in downtown Ithaca, New York, is a full-length portrait of a tall man with a beard, dressed in black frock coat, vest, and bowtie. A cursory glance might make you think you are looking at Abraham Lincoln, understandable since America's regard for our 16th president has resulted in ubiquitous tributes. Closer inspection of the painting however, shows significant beard and facial differences from the iconic "Honest Abe" figure we know so well.

In fact, Ezra Cornell, the figure on the wall and founder of Cornell University, has much more than superficial physical and sartorial links to Lincoln. Ezra Cornell supported Lincoln politically, and actually met him at a White House reception. Born two years before Lincoln, in Westchester County near New York City, Cornell's family moved to DeRuyter, New York, a few years later, a rural upstate region that held many of the frontier challenges facing the Lincoln family in Kentucky and later Indiana. Like Lincoln he had little formal schooling but shared a hunger for learning, and technology. He also knew poverty but through hard work and technical ingenuity became wealthy from his work with the newly invented telegraph. He was in the state legislature when the Morrill Land Grant Act was passed and with his own political guidance and generous financial contribution saw America's first institution that actually began as a university, as opposed to a college, built on his farmstead in Ithaca, New York. Cornell University, chartered in 1865, would become the youngest of the eight Ivy League schools. The first new building on the Cornell campus was Morrill Hall, named for Justin Morrill whose Land Grant Act allowed the creation of the University. In 1881 Lincoln Hall was built on campus to recognize his key role in the school's birth. Lincoln had signed the Land Grant Act that his predecessor had vetoed.

Lincoln also helped revolutionarily change American education. His predecessor, President Buchanan, had vetoed the Morrill Land Grant Act, an act that would have given federal land to the states which they could sell so they could build schools of agriculture and engineering to add professional and practical education to the classically focused education currently available. When the act was resubmitted in 1863 Lincoln readily signed it and Land Grant schools were established in all states in the nation. While most of these schools are state schools (Penn State, Michigan State, University of Massachusetts for example), two, Cornell University (later to become one of the eight Ivy League Schools) and MIT, are private schools founded by the Land Grant Act.

The act that Lincoln signed was similar to the one Buchanan had vetoed with one exception. Since the country was now in a Civil War, Military Science was added to the required curriculum. For many years all Land Grant Colleges at least offered ROTC.

AGES OR ANGELS?

Lincoln died in the Petersen Boarding House on the morning of April 15, after being shot the evening before across the street in Ford's Theatre. Secretary of War Edwin Stanton reportedly said, "Now he belongs to the ages." But at least one other witness thought it was, "Now he belongs to the angels." Stanton helped perpetuate his version. All we know for sure is the small room was full and everyone was weeping.

MARY TODD LINCOLN'S FRIEND AND CONFIDANTE

Mary Todd was raised in a slave-holding family in Lexington, Kentucky. They called them servants, not slaves. Nevertheless they were slaves. While living in the White House, Mary hired a talented seamstress, Elizabeth Keckley, a former slave who had purchased her own freedom. Mary became close to Keckley, especially after the death of her son, Willie Lincoln, and later her husband. They traveled together during a very difficult period in Mary's life. This aide and friend provided a great deal of assistance, often causing her to neglect her own business. It didn't end well. Keckley agreed to a book deal, which was ghostwritten and published. Because it included some of her conversations and letters, Mary was furious. She ended what was perhaps her closest friendship, and became more a recluse than ever.

CONTENTS OF LINCOLN'S POCKETS AT FORD'S THEATRE

When he was shot the contents of his pockets were placed in a box and given to his son Robert. Much later the box was passed on to Robert's daughter. It was given to the Library of Congress and made public in 1976. It contained one pair of gold-rimmed glasses and another pair of folding spectacles folded into a silver case; a small velvet eyeglass cleaner; an ivory pocketknife rimmed in silver; a monogrammed handkerchief; and a brown leather wallet lined with purple silk. The wallet contained a five-dollar Confederate bill with the Jefferson Davis image, and eight newspaper clippings. He was usually so maligned that when he saw an article that praised him, he often kept it.

Some recent historians have said that he also carried a letter from Eliza Gurney, a Quaker woman who, as part of a pacifist delegation of Quakers, had visited the White House several years before. He later wrote her a letter and she responded. Some say that her letter moved him so much that he kept it in his pocket the next two years.

THE JOHN WILKES BOOTH FAMILY CONNECTION

His death at the hands of John Wilkes Booth, one of the most famous actors in America, is accompanied with many ironies. Lincoln loved the theater and attended Ford's Theatre nine times. Ten days before he gave his historic speech in Gettysburg he, along with Mary and his sister-in-law, sat in his box at the theater to see John Wilkes Booth in *The Marble Heart*. At one point Booth was shaking his finger and delivering a tirade. Lincoln's sister-in-law remarked that he seemed to be directing it at Lincoln. Lincoln said, "He does seem to be looking at me pretty sharp, doesn't he?"

A month before the assassination Booth was secretly engaged

to Lucy Lambert Hale, the daughter of Senator John Hale. (Lincoln's oldest son Robert had once courted Lucy, and once was pulled from sure death at a railway station by Booth's older brother Edwin.) Lucy got Booth a VIP pass for Lincoln's second inaugural address and he was very close to the president during the speech. Most agree that Booth's first plan was to kidnap Lincoln and hold him for ransom, trading him for the thousands of Confederate prisoners in Northern prison camps. But after hearing a Lincoln talk from a White House window, two days after Lee's surrender, in which Lincoln mentioned black men getting the franchise (being able to vote), Booth turned to his companion and said, "He has given his last speech." Three days later he shot Abraham Lincoln at Ford's Theatre.

A SILENT ASSASSIN NOT NAMED BOOTH?

In 1962 a physician suggested that Lincoln might have had a genetic disease called Marfan syndrome. This was primarily because of his tall lanky appearance, shared by his mother. This theory was generally accepted for a number of years. But the disease seems to also include a weak heart and chest capacity, and relatively early death. Since Lincoln was considered one of the best athletes and strongest persons in his community, and he lived until he was murdered at 56, the Marfan theory is now questioned by many scientists.

However, in *The Physical Lincoln,* Dr. John Sotos suggests that if John Wilkes Booth hadn't murdered Lincoln he still would have been dead within a few months. Commentators have often talked about how extraordinarily rapid the Lincoln aging process was, based on pictures of his face from his election in 1860 until his death in 1865. The common assumption is that this was because of the pressures of his job, and of the war. In fact the changes in his appearance are even more startling. Dr. Sotos thinks that Lincoln was suffering from MEN2B (multiple endocrine neoplasia, type 2B), a rare disease that was eating his body away from within. He bolsters his argument with many supporting facts including the early deaths of three of Lincoln's children and of his mother, and their common symptoms.

Incidentally, Dr. Sotos also theorized that Mary Todd Lincoln suffered from Pernicious Anemia (PA, lack of vitamin B12), with symptoms including a regular pallor to her skin, fever, headaches, gait problems, abnormal sensations as if she were being stuck by needles, soreness to her mouth, swelling, shortness of breath and resting tachycardia. She started to show signs of hyper-vigilance, delusions, and hallucinations, but all with a kind of perceived clarity. Vitamin B12 deficiency shrinks the brain, leading to a significant decline in cognitive function, paranoia, and hallucinations. As she got older, the energetic woman who loved to read could no longer see well, and toward the end she became so weak and tired that she could barely move. Eventually, no longer able to speak, she communicated by blinking. We will never really know Mary Lincoln's condition, but we do know that today Pernicious Anemia is readily treated with medications.

LINCOLN LORE #22

THE WATCH WITH A MESSAGE

In the 1850s, Abraham Lincoln, then a successful lawyer in Springfield, purchased a fine pocket watch with an 18-carat gold case. After being elected Lincoln was in Washington and his watch was in a DC jewelry shop for repair. The Confederates had just fired on Fort Sumter and the watchmaker, Jonathan Dillon, unscrewed the dial and engraved a message mentioning the attack and saying, "Thank God we have a government." No one knew about this engraving except other watchmakers, who added comments over the years. One added the 1864 date, another wrote, "Jefferson Davis." Dillon told this story to *The New York Times* in 1906. In 2009 a descendant contacted the Smithsonian, where the watch was stored, and told them the story. They opened the watch and found the inscriptions.

LINCOLN LORE #23

ROBERT LINCOLN SEES HIS FATHER FOR THE LAST TIME

Robert, Lincoln's oldest son, was with his father when he died, the morning after he was shot in 1865. Lincoln and all his family, except Robert, who is buried in Arlington National Cemetery, are buried in Oak Ridge Cemetery in Springfield, Illinois.

Robert next saw his father in 1901, 36 years later. There had been a number of attempts to steal the body for ransom over the years so it was finally decided to entomb the body under concrete. Because some of the attempts at stealing the body had moved the casket, it was decided to open the casket to be sure it was actually Lincoln. The casket was opened and viewed by witnesses, including Robert, to be sure it was Lincoln. The body was instantly recognizable. He had been embalmed for the long trip back to Springfield with many stops and viewings along the way. One young boy in the viewing party said he had trouble sleeping for weeks after seeing the body. Witnesses were initially confused by some colored bits of cloth on his chest until they figured out it was from an American flag that had deteriorated. After the viewing Lincoln was buried under an impressive monument.

Large crowd watching crane lift box containing Abraham Lincoln's body. Courtesy of Library of Congress.

A FUTURE PRESIDENT VIEWS THE PASSING OF ANOTHER

A recent photographic discovery shows that seven-year-old Theodore Roosevelt and his brother watched as the Lincoln funeral procession went by the family home in New York City. His father knew the Lincolns well. When sworn into office decades later Roosevelt carried a lock of Lincoln's hair. Theodore Roosevelt and Lincoln are honored on Mt. Rushmore, as are Washington and Jefferson. President Roosevelt was the person who initiated the honoring of Lincoln's Centennial by putting his likeness on the U.S. penny in 1909.

WITNESS TO HISTORY, OR A JINX?

Four U.S. presidents have been assassinated: Abraham Lincoln (1865), James Garfield (1881), William McKinley (1901), and John F. Kennedy (1963). Lincoln's oldest son, Robert, was with his father when he died; Robert was Secretary of War and with President Garfield when he was shot at DC's Union Station; he was a special envoy and in Buffalo, New York, when McKinley died after being shot. He felt he was a jinx and refused any further government appointments. After JFK was assassinated he was buried not far from Robert in Arlington National Cemetery.

THE MAGNIFICENT LINCOLN MEMORIAL

Perhaps the most impressive, and certainly one of the most popular monuments in Washington, DC, did not have an easy birth. In 1867, two years after Lincoln's death, Congress submitted the first of many bills to build a monument to honor him. Questions of cost, design, and location were argued for years. A bill was finally passed in 1910, authorizing the Washington D.C. Commission of Fine Arts to build a memorial.

Selecting its site was also filled with controversy. Many locations were considered but they finally accepted the suggestion of John Hay, one of Lincoln's presidential secretaries, and former Secretary of State. He urged a location called the Potomac Flats, saying it was ideal because the monument should stand alone, dignified and serene. Though a swampy area at the time, it has proven to be the perfect location.

Architect Henry Bacon was chosen to design a memorial to house a statue of Lincoln. He conceived of a Parthenon-type Greek temple. Renowned sculptor Daniel Chester French was Bacon's recommendation to do the statue itself, and French was accepted. Henry Bacon and Daniel Chester French had also collaborated on another Lincoln statue, one begun on his birthday in 1909, Lincoln's centennial. This monument, a standing Lincoln, was commissioned by the Abraham Lincoln Memorial Association of Lincoln, Nebraska, stands on the ground of the State Capitol and was dedicated in 1912.

Work on the Lincoln Memorial began on Lincoln's birthday, February 12, 1914. [The prototype casting of French's seated Lincoln statue is in the rotunda of Lincoln's Tomb in Springfield, Illinois.] During construction one major design change was made. It was decided that the original 10-foot Lincoln would be lost in the vast Memorial chamber, and the seated Lincoln is now 19 feet tall.

Inscribed on the wall behind Lincoln is:

IN THIS TEMPLE
AS IN THE HEARTS OF THE PEOPLE
FOR WHOM HE SAVED THE UNION
THE MEMORY OF ABRAHAM LINCOLN
IS ENSHRINED FOREVER

Lincoln statue under construction in the Lincoln Memorial. Courtesy of Library of Congress.

On its walls are two of his most iconic speeches, *The Gettysburg Address* and the *Second Inaugural*.

The Memorial was dedicated on May 30, 1922, with his only living son, 79-year-old Robert, in attendance.

The Lincoln Memorial has been included as a backdrop in many movies, and has been the location for many historic events. In 1939 it was the site of Marian Anderson's public concert after the Daughters of the American Revolution refused to allow an African-American to sing in Constitution Hall. In 1963 Martin Luther King, Jr., delivered his legendary "I Have a Dream" speech from there, paying tribute to Lincoln and his belief that all men are created equal. [Opening that speech with, "Five score years ago, a great American in whose symbolic shadow we stand, signed the Emancipation Proclamation."] In 2019, President Donald Trump delivered an historic Independence Day speech from the Lincoln Memorial.

There seems to be no basis to the myth that Lincoln's hands are secretly sending a sign-language message.

[While there are many Lincoln statues, around this country and the world (see page 214), and the Washington Lincoln Memorial is arguably the most admired, there are at least three other sculptors that should be recognized.

During Lincoln's presidency a talented teenage sculptress, Vinnie Ream, actually visited the Executive Mansion and the president would "sit" for her, in the mornings for five months. She created a bust of Lincoln. After his death Congress offered a commission for a full-size statue of Lincoln, to be made of white Carrara marble. While only 18 years old,

Vinnie Ream won the commission and began work on her creation, both in the U.S. and Europe. She was 23 when the completed work was unveiled in the United States Capitol Rotunda, where it remains. Whenever prominent personages lie in state in the Rotunda, for example JFK in 1963, Abraham Lincoln is there looking down.

Augustus Saint-Gaudens (1848–1907), a prolific sculptor, created many highly regarded Lincoln statues. In 1887 he completed *The Standing Lincoln*, for Lincoln Park in Chicago (a replica stands at Lincoln's Tomb in Springfield, and another in Parliament Square, London.) For the Lincoln Centennial in 1909 he created a seated *Abraham Lincoln, The Head of State*, which is in Grant Park in Chicago, IL.

From 1927 to 1941, sculptor Gutzon Borglum and his son Lincoln Borglum, created the magnificent Mount Rushmore tribute to George Washington, Thomas Jefferson, Theodore Roosevelt, and Abraham Lincoln. A bronze replica of Borglum's head of Lincoln is part of the majestic Lincoln Tomb in Springfield, Illinois]

SECRET SERVICE, TOO LITTLE, TOO LATE

I n the mid-1800s one third of U.S. currency in circulation was counterfeit. On the day Lincoln was shot he signed a bill authorizing the creation of a Secret Service within the Treasury Department to address the counterfeiting problem. It wasn't until two more presidential assassinations (Garfield and McKinley) that Congress, in 1902, added protecting the president to the mission of the Secret Service. It is now part of Homeland Security.

THE PITCHMAN, DID HE SAY IT, OR NOT?

Arguably, one of the most commonly quoted "Lincoln-isms" is, "You can fool some of the people all of the time, you can fool all of the people some of the time, but you can't fool all the people all of the time." It is a catchy phrase, but there is no record of Lincoln having actually uttered it. It first appeared a decade or so after his death with products quoting it and attributing it to him. It became very popular in advertisements.

In 1960 an album by stand-up comic Bob Newhart became an instant best seller with a bit called, "Abe Lincoln vs. Madison Ave." Newhart plays what today would be called a "Branding Agent" talking on the phone to a not very bright Lincoln in Gettysburg. Among other information and suggestions Newhart tells "Abe" that he has to get his famous quote correct. Lincoln apparently kept saying, "You can fool all the people all of the time..."

We can all agree that even if he didn't say it, he could have, and perhaps he should have.

The Merchants, who used the so-called Lincoln quote in their ads, were just the beginning.

While Lincoln became a very successful lawyer, he was an honest but failed businessman, paying off his store debts over many years. Nevertheless, this has not stopped commercial enterprises from using him as a very effective marketing "spokesman."

Lincoln, with his top hat and beard, is readily identifiable. He shares this fact with few other American historical figures. The short list, those with unique physical or sartorial characteristics, include Teddy Roosevelt and Ben Franklin. But most others, George Washington, John Adams, Thomas Jefferson, Alexander Hamilton, for instance, do not. Lincoln also enjoys a positive persona, one of honesty, hard work, compassion and being self-made. He may now be more popular and well known than he ever was.

For these reasons, hundreds of companies and products have capitalized on that Lincoln appeal. His name and/or image is on coffee mugs, tobacco products, T-shirts, cologne, Band-Aids – you name it. There is even a Mr. Lincoln rose, which, "was for many years the most popular and the best of red hybrid tea rose varieties."

Since 1917 there have been Lincoln cars. Henry Leland, the creator of the Cadillac, named his company the Lincoln Motor Company to honor his favorite president. In 1922 he sold the company to Ford and it has been a luxury brand for Ford ever since. Ironically, it was only in 2013 that Lincoln Motors began using Abraham Lincoln images in its advertising.

[In 2011 a popular novel became a film, *The Lincoln Lawyer*. It featured a slick defense attorney who conducted his business out of a luxurious Lincoln Town Car. The star of the movie later did ads for the automobile, joining the Abraham Lincoln persona, which occasionally appeared in the commercials, in touting the Lincoln automobile.]

Perhaps the only company using his name with family permission is the Lincoln Financial Group. In 1905 they wrote to Abraham Lincoln's primary living relative, his son Robert, asking to use the name for its new company. Robert sent them a letter authorizing them to do so.

LINCOLN LORE #29

NO ADONIS, HE

Walt Whitman, one of America's most acclaimed poets, would frequently see Lincoln on the streets of Washington. They had a nodding acquaintance. Commenting on Lincoln's looks, Whitman wrote in a letter, "Lincoln had a face, like a Hoosier Michelangelo, so awful ugly it becomes beautiful."

[Walt Whitman reported that he saw some beautiful lilacs on the day of Lincoln's assassination and many think he wrote "When Lilacs Last in the Dooryard Bloomed" in honor of Lincoln. Today the "President Lincoln" Lilac variety is very hardy and popular. Whitman also wrote the moving poem "O Captain! My Captain!" to honor the slain president; see Lincoln Lore #54.]

After his election to president, Lincoln left for Washington by train to be sworn in. At one of the many stops along the way, Pittsburgh, the *Post* editor wrote: "Mr. Lincoln [is not] as ungainly in personal appearance, nor as ugly in the face as he has been represented....He is by no means a handsome man, [but] his facial angles would not break a looking glass."

Lincoln knew he wasn't physically attractive and developed many ways of using this to his advantage. When addressing an audience, especially if it included women, he would say, "You came to see me and I came to see you, and I know I am getting the better part of that deal."

During his debates with Douglas he responded to being called "two-faced" (i.e., lying) by saying, "My opponent has called me two-faced. I leave it to you, my audience, if I had two faces would I wear this one?"

He would also welcome an audience for being there by telling the story of the young man on horseback who met a woman going the opposite way. In passing she observed, "I must say you are the homeliest person I've ever met in my life." The young man replied, "That may be true ma'am, but there is nothing I can do about it." She replied, "You could have stayed home!"

Finally, he would tell the story of meeting a very homely man. The man looked at him, pulled a pistol and shoved it under Lincoln's nose, saying, "I always said that if I met a man uglier than myself I would shoot him on the spot." Lincoln replied, "Shoot away, if I am uglier than you I want to die."

DON'T CALL ME ABE

His friends called him Abraham, or more commonly just Lincoln. He earned the "Honest Abe" nickname early, and it, along with "Rail-Splitter" (because so much of his youth was spent chopping logs into "rails" for fencing), was used in political campaigns. Mary, his wife, called him Father. Many of his ardent supporters of both races called him "Father Abraham." After signing the Emancipation Proclamation in 1863 he became the "Great Emancipator." His secretaries in the White House, John Nicolay and John Hay, respectfully called him the "Tycoon" (not to his face). He usually signed his name, "A. Lincoln." He was not called Abe by any friends or colleagues.

ILLINOIS, LAND OF LINCOLN — OR IS IT?

The Hutchinsons, an Abolitionist family from New England, helped Lincoln get elected to his first term as president in 1860 by writing and performing their song, "Lincoln and Liberty."

> Hurrah for the choice of the nation
>
> Our chieftain so brave and so true
>
> We'll go for the great reformation
>
> For Lincoln and Liberty too!
>
> We'll go for the son of Kentucky
>
> The Hero of Hoosier-dom through

The pride of the Suckers so lucky

Lincoln and Liberty too.

A Hoosier was the nickname for someone who lived in Indiana and a resident of Illinois was known as a Sucker (it was not considered an insult). So while Illinois has been very successful in claiming itself the "Land of Lincoln," the song reminds us that Lincoln was born and spent his first seven years in Kentucky, the next fourteen years in Indiana, and the next thirty years in Illinois.

Every 50 years the reverse side of the Lincoln penny, first minted in 1909, the 100th anniversary of his birth, is changed. On the 200th anniversary of his birth, in 2009, four special edition pennies were minted. These special editions had backs each showing one of the four places Lincoln had lived: Kentucky, Indiana, Illinois, and Washington, DC.

So while all three states and the District of Columbia claim Lincoln, and have historical sites worth visiting, Illinois may have won the PR battle.

A PENNY, OR MAYBE A "FIN," FOR YOUR THOUGHTS

President Teddy Roosevelt was the person who initiated the honoring of Lincoln by suggesting putting his likeness on the U.S. cent. This coin was first minted in 1909, the centennial celebration of Lincoln's 1809 birth, and soon began to be called the "penny" after the English coin.

This cent was the first American coin portraying a real person on its face, and, from 1959 to 2009, was the only U.S. coin with the same person on both sides (during that period the reverse side, which has been changed every 50 years, showed the Lincoln Memorial with the seated Lincoln visible between the columns).

The obverse or heads (front) side of the coin was designed by Victor David Brenner, as was the first reverse or tails (back) side. "In God we trust," "Liberty," and Lincoln's head are on the front, and "E Pluribus Unum" ("Out of many, one") and "United States of America" are on the back.

The artist, Victor David Brenner, put his initials, VDB, on some of the earlier cents in various sizes and those coins have become extremely valuable. The coins have been minted each year since 1909, with the year printed on the front.

The coins have been minted in the Philadelphia Mint, the Denver Mint, the San Francisco Mint, and the West Point Mint. The mintmark, when used, appears under the year. Most of these coins were minted in Philadelphia and have no mintmark, but some were minted in Denver and have a "D" under the year, and some in San Francisco and have an "S" under the year. From 1974 to 1986 the West Point Mint produced pennies, and like Philadelphia, used no mintmark. In 2017 the Philadelphia Mint, the oldest mint in this country, celebrated its 225th anniversary by putting a "P" on all its pennies for that year.

While initially composed primarily of copper, the composition of the cent has changed over the years based on the price of various metals. In 1943, in the midst of the Second World War, the cent was made of steel and covered with zinc, which made it silver in color – some called it white.

As mentioned, the back of the cent has been changed every 50 years. From 1909 to 1958 the back featured wheat stalks up the sides of the coin. From 1959 to 2008, the back of the cent showed the Lincoln Memorial. In 2009 (his 200th birthday) there were four different backs, one for each of the places Lincoln lived: Kentucky, Indiana, Illinois, and Washington, DC. Since 2010 the back has been the US Shield.

Today it costs more to make a cent than its value. One wonders how much longer the country will mint cents. The Lincoln "penny" may soon be an historical artifact.

The five-dollar bill (or "fin" in slang) has been around since 1861. It was originally considered a "Demand Note" and featured Alexander Hamilton. Since then there have been many size and design changes, including a 1914 five-dollar Federal Reserve Note with Lincoln on the front.

The present-day Lincoln five-dollar bill with the Lincoln Memorial on the back was first introduced in 1929. It has been modified many times for currency security purposes but still features Lincoln on the front and his Memorial on the back.

LINCOLN LOGS AND LOG CABIN QUILTS

In the early 1900s the world-famous architect Frank Lloyd Wright was hired to build what would become one of the greatest hotels in the world, the Imperial Hotel in Tokyo, Japan. He hired his son, John Lloyd Wright, as chief assistant. Because of the danger of earthquakes the architect had developed an ingenious system of interlocking log beams, allowing the building to sway but not collapse. [The hotel was tested in a major quake in 1923, which devastated most of Tokyo but left the hotel standing.]

John and his father had a falling-out before the hotel was built; desperate to earn money, John used the hotel's blueprint to design a toy using small, notched wooden pieces. In 1918 he began marketing his product and in 1920 received a patent for a "toy-cabin construction" set.

His company, J. L. Wright Manufacturing, provided instructions on how to build Uncle Tom's Cabin, along with Abraham Lincoln's cabin in the original set. Later sets were larger and more complex, and "Lincoln Logs" became very popular.

In 1999 the National Toy Hall of Fame inducted both Lincoln Logs and John Lloyd Wright. In September 2014 the distributor announced that the toy's production was returning from China to the United States. Today there are numerous toy construction sets, many more sophisticated than Lincoln Logs, but Lincoln Logs remain popular with young creative minds.

Quilting has a long history of both practicality and enjoyment, with quilts used for warmth, comfort, decoration, and even burial. Traceable back to the days of Egyptian Pharaohs, quilts have a rich history. Once limited to the rich who could afford the fabrics and the needed labor, they became more common as fabric-making technology advanced. Quilts served a multitude of useful and often essential purposes, but also became a relaxing and even social pastime for women during America's colonial, frontier, and Civil War periods. A particular block pattern on the quilt is called the Log Cabin pattern, and was sometimes even called the Lincoln Log Cabin pattern during Lincoln's presidency, and after his death.

NO "STENO POOL" FOR MR. L.

During his presidency Lincoln had three secretaries: John Nicolay, John Hay, and William Stoddard.

John Nicolay was born in Germany, moving to America when he was six. He lived in Illinois and became active in state politics. He served as Lincoln's secretary during the 1860 presidential campaign, and after the election was officially appointed first secretary. He moved to Washington with Lincoln, lived in the Executive Mansion, and served as chief secretary until Lincoln's death.

John Hay was born in Indiana, graduated from Brown University, and while studying law in Springfield got to know both Lincoln and Nicolay. During the presidential campaign he helped Nicolay, who after the successful election suggested he also be brought to DC to assist with clerical demands. He became the "unofficial" second secretary (his salary charged to the Department of the Interior), and, with Nicolay, lived in the Executive Mansion, serving until Lincoln's death.

William Stoddard ran a paper in Illinois and helped Lincoln's campaign. After Lincoln was in office a few months it was agreed that the overwhelming correspondence required more help and Stoddard was hired. He became the third secretary and served until 1864. He did not live in the White House. Of Lincoln's three secretaries, Stoddard got along best with Mary Lincoln, and assisted her too. [Stoddard opened all her mail before she saw it, eliminating the too frequently threatening, vile, and hateful.]

After Lincoln's death Nicolay and Hay collaborated on a multi-volume series, *Abraham Lincoln: A History*.

Stoddard wrote many books, including *Inside the White House in War Times*. He reportedly said, "I am convinced that when someone in America goes mad [insane] the first thing he does is write a letter to the president."

LINCOLN'S BRANCHLESS FAMILY TREE

Lincoln's father and mother, Tom and Nancy, had three children: one son who died at birth; a daughter, Sarah, who died, with her baby, in childbirth at 21; and Abraham. Only son Abraham lived to adulthood, dying at 56.

Abraham and Mary had four sons: Robert, Eddie, Willie, and Thomas (called "Tad" because his father thought he looked like a tadpole when born).

Only Robert lived to adulthood. Eddie died at three (in 1850); Willie at eleven (in 1862); and Tad at eighteen (in 1871).

Robert (died 1926) and wife Mary Harlin Lincoln (died

1937) had three children: Jack (officially, Abraham II), who died in his teens, in 1890); Mary, called Mamie; and Jessie.

Mamie married Charles Isham and had a son, Lincoln Isham.

Mamie died in 1938; her son Lincoln in 1971.

Jessie (died 1948) married Warren Beckwith and had two children, Mary (called Peggy) (died in 1975), and Robert.

Robert Beckwith, the last of the Tom and Nancy Lincoln/ Abraham and Mary Lincoln line, died in 1985.

Lincoln family in 1861. Courtesy of Library of Congress.

LINCOLN "FIRSTS"

- Lincoln was first person to use photographs in a presidential political campaign, and during his White House years.

- First president born outside the original thirteen colonies (see Lincoln Lore #1).

- Tallest president.

- First president with facial hair (see Lincoln Lore #12).

- Only president with a patent (see Lincoln Lore #7)..

- Only active president to visit front lines in a war (see Lincoln Lore #14).

- First real person depicted on an American coin, the 1909 Lincoln penny. The reverse side of the penny is changed every 50 years. From 1959 to 2008 the reverse of the penny shows the Lincoln Memorial. The seated figure of Lincoln in the Memorial is slightly visible, making this the only American coin with the same person on both sides of the coin (see Lincoln Lore #32).

- First Republican president.

- The first president to utilize the telegraph as means of communication, some call it his "T-Mails."

- His administration instituted a National Bank, paper currency, Income Tax, and Thanksgiving as a national holiday; opened the West through the Homestead Act; created Land Grant Colleges (Agriculture and Engineering) in every state; guaranteed transcontinental rail transportation with the Pacific Railway Act; and created Yosemite National Park.

- First president to be assassinated.

LINCOLN AND JOHN F. KENNEDY, COINCIDENCES

After the 1963 assassination of John Kennedy, the fourth U.S. president slain in office, a list began to circulate about the coincidences between his life and death and that of Abraham Lincoln. Both deaths shocked the nation and both friends and many political foes mourned their loss, and tried to make some sense of it.

Some of these "coincidences" are indeed interesting. Others are a bit of a stretch, and some just wrong.

- Abraham Lincoln was elected to Congress in 1846. John F. Kennedy was elected to Congress in 1946.

**Abraham Lincoln, Congressman-elect from Illinois. Oldest known photo
taken of Lincoln. (1846) Courtesy of Library of Congress.**

- Lincoln was elected president in 1860. Kennedy was elected president in 1960.

- The names Lincoln and Kennedy each contain seven letters.

- Both were particularly concerned with civil rights.

- Both lost a child while living in the White House.

- Both were shot on a Friday.

- Both were shot in the head.

- Both were assassinated by Southerners and succeeded by Southerners.

- Both successors were named Johnson.

- Andrew Johnson, who succeeded Lincoln, was born in 1808. Lyndon B. Johnson, who succeeded Kennedy, was born in 1908.

- Both assassins, John Wilkes Booth and Lee Harvey Oswald, were known by their three names.

- Both names are comprised of fifteen letters.

- Booth ran from the theater and was caught in a warehouse (actually a tobacco barn). Oswald ran from a warehouse and was caught in a theater (actually a movie theater).

- Both Booth and Oswald were assassinated before their trials.

- Lincoln's oldest son, Robert, was with him when he died, and is buried near Kennedy in Arlington.

Some coincidences that are on most lists don't bear scrutiny too well:

- Lincoln's secretary, named Kennedy, warned him not to go to the theatre. Kennedy's secretary, named Lincoln, warned him not to go to Dallas.

  ⊳ While Kennedy did have a secretary named Lincoln, she went to Dallas with him, and there is no record of her having warned Kennedy. Lincoln had three secretaries, none named Kennedy.

- John Wilkes Booth, who killed Lincoln, was born in 1839. Lee Harvey Oswald, who killed Kennedy, was born in 1939.

  ⊳ Booth was actually born in 1838.

ICONIC SPEECHES, A CENTURY APART

L incoln was one of the finest writers and orators that this country has ever produced. John F. Kennedy's acclaimed speechwriter, Ted Sorenson, has said that perhaps the greatest presidential speechwriter in this country's history is Abraham Lincoln, who of course wrote his own speeches.

Many now say that Lincoln's most powerful and eloquent speech is his "With malice toward none, and with charity for all" second inaugural speech. It was a moving, sermon-like attempt to heal a divided nation at the end of its bloody Civil War.

But for sheer poetic beauty, Lincoln's Gettysburg Address stands alone. In November 1863, he was invited to participate

Lincoln spotted in photo of the
dedication of Gettysburg cemetery.
Courtesy of Library of Congress.

in the dedication of the Veterans Cemetery at the site of one
of the bloodiest battles of the Civil War. The main speaker at
the event was Edward Everett, known as one of the greatest
orators of his era. He spoke for two hours. Then Lincoln
spoke, for less than three minutes. He was finished before the
press had time to set up their cameras. Like all his speeches,
he worked very hard at preparing and polishing his remarks.
His opening, "Four score and seven years ago, our fathers
brought forth on this continent," became legendary, not only
for its beauty, but more importantly its message, which came
from the founding fathers – all men are created equal. He

wrote out five copies of this speech: two before it was delivered, and three after. All five copies have minor differences, with the last three including the phrase "under God." The first two copies are in the Library of Congress. The others are in the Lincoln Museum in Springfield, at Cornell University, and in the Lincoln Bedroom in the White House.

One hundred years later, in November 1963, Martin Luther King Jr. delivered his eloquent, nonviolent demand for civil rights in one of the great speeches of all time to thousands in front of the Lincoln Memorial in Washington, DC. He opened this speech by paying tribute to Lincoln's Gettysburg speech by saying, "Five score years ago, a great American, in whose symbolic shadow we stand, signed the Emancipation Proclamation." His "I Have a Dream" speech will also deservedly go down in history.

LINCOLN LORE #39

NO RUSH TO JUDGMENT, LET JUSTICE PREVAIL

In late 1862, Lincoln, in the midst of dealing with continuing Union military disasters, handling a combative cabinet, and agonizing over the Emancipation Proclamation, struggled over another matter. More than 300 Indians had been convicted of war crimes in Minnesota's Great Sioux Uprising, now termed the "Dakota-U.S. Conflict." Hundreds of Indians, white settlers, and soldiers had died during this uprising. The U.S. Army, after ending the conflict, set up a commission that condemned 303 Dakota men to be hanged. Lincoln needed to decide whether to allow their executions to go forward.

Under Chief Little Crow, the Dakota had raged across the countryside with a fury, following mistreatment by government agents and rumors that previously promised gold and credit would not be forthcoming. During the first four days of the rampage, four to eight hundred white settlers were slaughtered and their fields and farms burned, causing panic to spread across Minnesota.

After the U.S. Army suppressed the uprising it established a commission that ended up sentencing 303 Dakota men to be hanged. The commission acted very quickly, conducting 392 trials, including 40 in one day, over a five-week period. Although the charges varied from rape to murder to theft, most Dakota were accused of participating in battles. One man who helped in the evidence-gathering process reported, "The plan was adopted to subject all the grown men, with a few exceptions to an investigation of the commission, trusting that the innocent would make their innocence appear."

The military wanted to begin the executions immediately, but the sentences required presidential review. After the names of the condemned were telegraphed to Lincoln, he responded by asking for "the full and complete record of these convictions" and to identify "the more guilty and influential of the culprits."

"Anxious to not act with so much clemency as to encourage another outbreak" but also seeking justice, Lincoln disregarded the white population's revenge-seeking and began to review the trial records and decide the defendants' fates. Lincoln was deluged with telegrams and letters from folks on both sides of the issue. Clergymen, Army officers, and politicians came to the White House, offering advice. Lincoln patiently listened to their evidence and counsel.

Lincoln issued his decision on December 6, 1862 – in his own handwriting – allowing the execution of only 39 of the 303 condemned Dakota. Twenty-nine of the group had been convicted of murder, three of having "shot" someone, two for taking part in "massacres," and one for mutilation. Only two had been convicted of rape, Lincoln related to the Senate.

This was not the first time Lincoln saved an Indian's life. One story from Lincoln's Black Hawk War service in 1832 involves an old Potawotami Indian who wandered into Captain Lincoln's camp. Lincoln's men assumed him a spy and wanted to kill him. The story goes that Lincoln threw himself between the Native American and the men's muskets, knocking their weapons upward and protecting the Indian.

LINCOLN LORE #40

STAR OF STAGE, SCREEN, AND TV

MOVIES

Lincoln has been mentioned and often shown in many films, for instance the groundbreaking *Birth of a Nation*, a 1915 silent movie that unfortunately was outstandingly racially offensive. In the epic *Gone with the Wind* (1939) Scarlett O'Hara, newly widowed and with her fellow Georgians devastated by the war, said at a fund-raising Confederate Ball, "I'm going to dance, and dance. Tonight I wouldn't mind dancing with Abraham Lincoln himself." [Scarlett perhaps should have talked to Mary Lincoln. Mary Lincoln joked that when she first met Lincoln, at a social gathering in Springfield, he asked her to dance by saying, "I would like to dance with you in the worst way." She would say that that is exactly how he ended up dancing with her, "In the worst way."]

In the 1935 movie *Littlest Rebel* Shirley Temple actually sat on Lincoln's lap in his office as they shared an apple he was cutting and discussed a pardon for her father, a Confederate officer. A moving scene, and one that accurately displayed his compassion and wisdom.

EXCELLENT FULL-LENGTH MOVIES ABOUT HIM

- *Abraham Lincoln*, 1930, by D.W. Griffith, written by Stephen Vincent Benet, starring Walter Huston

- *Young Mr. Lincoln*, 1939, by John Ford, starring Henry Fonda

- *Abe Lincoln in Illinois*, 1940, from Robert E. Sherwood's play, starring Raymond Massey

- *Lincoln*, 2012, by Steven Spielberg, starring Daniel Day-Lewis and Sally Field. Based on Doris Kearns Goodwin's bestselling book, *Team of Rivals*.

LINCOLN MOVIES I'VE MANAGED TO AVOID

- *Abraham Lincoln: Vampire Hunter*, 2012

- *Abraham Lincoln vs. Zombies*, 2012

TV AND RADIO

Many, including:

- *Abraham Lincoln,* 1938, aired on the Orson Welles radio show *Mercury Theatre*

- Abraham Lincoln,** 1952, presented on TV's Studio One

- *Sandburg's Lincoln,* 1974, with Hal Holbrook; TV mini-series

- *The Last of Mrs. Lincoln,* 1976, TV adaptation of a stage play, starring Julie Harris

- *Abraham Lincoln,* Biography, History Channel

- *The Blue and the Gray,* 1982, with Gregory Peck; TV mini-series

- *Lincoln,* 1988, with Sam Waterston (based on Gore Vidal's novel)

- *Lincoln,* 1992, PBS TV presentation

- *Tad,* 1995, TV movie, Kris Kristofferson as Lincoln

- *Killing Lincoln,* 2013, TV movie, narrated by Tom Hanks

PLAYS

Abraham Lincoln, by John Drinkwater (an Englishman),

---

*   based on John Drinkwater's play
**   based on John Drinkwater's play

opened in England in 1918 and on Broadway in 1919. In 1938 Orson Welles put it on radio's *Mercury Theatre of the Air*. In 1924 a two-reel sound film version was made. In 1952 it was presented on TV's *Studio One* (actor James Dean played a small but significant role).

Abe Lincoln in Illinois, by Robert E. Sherwood, opened in 1938. It won the Pulitzer Prize for Drama in 1939. Raymond Massey played Lincoln and repeated the role in the movie version in 1940.

There have been innumerable other plays about Lincoln and/or his wife Mary. The Lincoln Presidential Library and Museum in Springfield, Illinois, includes a theater where different Lincoln-themed plays are presented.

Homer, a small town in central New York, celebrated the bicentennial of Lincoln's birth in 2009 by putting on a short, locally written play called *Freedom*. I was fortunate enough to play the part of Lincoln as it depicted his connection with three Homer residents who served him during the civil war. William Stoddard, his third secretary; Francis Carpenter, a talented artist who actually lived in the White House a short while as he was completing the *First Reading of the Emancipation Proclamation of President Lincoln* painting; and Eli DeVoe, a detective who uncovered a plot to assassinate Lincoln. [Homer is also the birthplace of Andrew White, the first president of Cornell University, the Ivy League school created by Lincoln's signing of the Morrill Land Grant Act.]

Some Lincoln re-enactors, often members of a group called ALP ("The Association of Lincoln Presenters"), market well-rehearsed programs to interested audiences. Occasionally these performances will also include someone portraying Mary Lincoln.

Scholastic Resources provides three Abraham Lincoln Reader's Theater scripts to elementary schools: *Holding the Nation Together*; *Will the Real Abraham Lincoln Please Stand Up?*, and *The Ballad of Abraham Lincoln*.

"MY BEST FRIEND IS THE PERSON WHO WILL GIVE ME A BOOK I HAVE NOT READ."

Today we take libraries for granted. Lincoln was not so fortunate. As Noah Webster said a few years before Lincoln's birth, "There are not more than three or four tolerable libraries in America and these are extremely imperfect." That was certainly true in rural Kentucky, Indiana, and Illinois, where Lincoln grew up. But this did not deter him. He read all the time and this sometimes got him into trouble. His father thought his reading interfered with his work assignments. Sometimes of course, it did. His father taught him to work, but he didn't teach him to like it. He taught himself to read, and always loved it. Friends said that after he was 12 or so they never saw him without a book in his hand or in his back pocket.

As he wrote in the copybook of a young friend:

> *Good boys who to their books apply*
> *Will make great men by and by*

He quickly figured out that what he wanted to know was in books and that his best friends were those that provided him books to read.

Probably his favorite book, not only because of its message, but also because of the wonderful way words and ideas were expressed, was the Bible. Both his birth mother and his stepmother shared with him their love for this book. His sister and he learned to read with the help of Dilworth's *Speller*, and also both enjoyed *Aesop's Fables*. Although his father became frustrated by his reading, he was grateful that his father brought home *Pilgrim's Progress*, thinking young Abraham would enjoy it and he did. His stepmother brought a few books with her when she married his father. *Robinson Crusoe* and *The Arabian Nights* (especially "Sinbad the Sailor") enthralled him.

Stories of great men also fascinated him, and he loved reading Ben Franklin's autobiography. Even his father enjoyed it when Abraham read that book aloud to him. *The Life of Washington* by Parson Weems helped ignite his life-long interest in our first president. Later he borrowed another book about Washington (by David Ramsay), and after inadvertently ruining it found out the real cost of learning. It took him several days to work off the value of the book, but he considered it well worth it. The *Etymological Dictionary* helped him build his vocabulary.

While it is true he did not spend much time in a classroom (he estimated no more than a year in total), some good books were being used in the schools and he would borrow them when he could. One of his favorites was Murrays's *English Reader*. It contained extracts from many famous writers. He also liked books about history.

At sixteen he read Lessons in Elocution, and used to practice public speaking in the woods near his home, sometimes to neighboring children. This helped what he had earlier learned in *Practical Discourses*. He began calling his reading in the woods my "Forest College." Some of his neighbors called this, "Abe's Brush College."

It would be a mistake, though, to conclude that he only read classic literature. There were many gazettes and badly written, some called them trashy, books on adventure and such. He couldn't afford the $1.50 many of them cost but he borrowed them whenever possible.

Books to him were not only an escape from a hard life but also a way for him to better himself. He did not want to live as his father did and was determined to learn as much as he could and to be able to effectively express himself, so that he might do something else. He wasn't sure what, but he knew there had to be something better out there for him. Much of this reading was to help him improve economically. He studied technical books so he could work as a surveyor. Then he studied law so he could become a lawyer. Later he read Euclid as a learning exercise.

Growing up he read Shakespeare, Robert Burns, Thomas Paine, Voltaire, and Edward Gibbon, and, as an adult, enjoyed the writings of Edgar Allan Poe.

As a young man he served as postmaster in New Salem, Illinois. This job didn't pay very much but did allow him to read the newspapers and magazines that came for local residents. It was also in New Salem that he made a friend, Jack Kelso, who shared his love of Shakespeare and Burns. Another friend, Mentor Graham, was the schoolmaster. He helped him with his study of calculus and law. James Rutledge of New Salem organized a debating society where young people could hone public speaking skills. These debates gave Lincoln a chance to practice what he had started back in Indiana.

His first law book, read as a youth, contained the statutes of Indiana, the Declaration of Independence, the Constitution, and the Northwest Ordinance with its prohibition of slavery. [see Lincoln Lore #3] He later read Blackstone's commentaries on English common law

His third and last law partner, William Herndon, complained that his reading aloud in their office was disturbing. Lincoln had found that by reading aloud he learned from two senses, not only seeing the words but hearing them too. Herndon sometimes had to leave the room when Lincoln did this. This habit of reading aloud may have been acquired when he was a youngster in what were called "blab" schools. These one-room schoolhouses would have children of different ages and grade levels reading aloud at the same time. One of the favorite books of his youth, because of the excerpted stories it contained, was the *English Reader*. It stressed reading these stories aloud.

He was well aware that his education was less than it should be. In 1847, after being elected to Congress he filled out the House information form by listing his education as "defective." It was clear to him that the only way to remedy this defect was by reading. The Libraries of Congress and the Supreme Court were like goldmines to him. He used to tie a number of books in a bandana handkerchief and carry them on a cane back to his boarding house.

Just after being elected president he checked out *The States-man's Manual* from the Illinois State Library. It contained every inaugural address from Washington to Polk. Before leaving for Washington, DC, he gave away his personal library. He prized books for their content, not as objects. During the Civil War he borrowed over 125 books on many different subjects from the Library of Congress. He also enjoyed the "dime" novels read by the soldiers. The comical books of Artemus Ward and Petroleum Vesuvius Nasby helped him get through some of the worst moments of the war. He knew, "that if I didn't laugh I would almost surely cry."

In his youth he began the lifelong practice of submitting letters and articles to newspapers. Also, he never missed an opportunity to speak in public. To understand and express ideas had always been important to him.

He also enjoyed poetry and tried his hand at writing a few poems. While interesting to read they do not measure up to the quality of his prose.

As for books about Lincoln, it is impossible to count them all. The total is well over 16,000. It has been said that no one has been the subject of more books except possibly Jesus Christ. In 2012 the Ford's Theatre Centre for Education and Leadership in Washington, DC, constructed a three-story tower of books about Lincoln.

I recall seeing an article written by an academic in the 1930s saying that everything that could be said about Lincoln had been said, and nothing more need be written. But Lincoln books continue to pour forth – a new book seems to be published every week.

I am often asked what is my favorite Lincoln book. My response has become, "The latest one I am currently reading." So many writers find a special niche or personal characteristic that gives the reader an intriguing new look at him.

I will mention some other early books, those written within a half-century or so of his death. Then I will mention some books in which the authors have taken a unique, perhaps even controversial, focus. It is clear that some writers got very personally involved with the Lincoln persona.

That includes some Lincoln haters, and yes, just as when he was alive, there are those who consider him undeserving of the iconic historic status he has achieved. Using selective research, some truths, and some half-truths, these writers paint Lincoln as a racist, a war-monger, a dictator, and an all-around bad guy. They completely ignore his growth as a man and a statesman, and put nothing into context. These books deserve the obscurity they have achieved.

Finally I will list a few of the best Lincoln books of the last half-century. There are just too many to do proper justice to them all. Most of my Lincoln readings have been histories, but I have found that a good novelist can describe the historic period so vividly that though the plot be fictionalized, an understanding of that time can be understood as no pure history can ever really do. This assumes the writer is as good a historian as novelist. An example is:

- *Lincoln* (1984), by Gore Vidal

  ⊳ While the plot is fictitious the characters are real and the reader gets a vivid, almost shocking, sense of the sights and smells of the Washington of that time.

FIRST BOOKS

Lincoln was shot on April 14, 1865, a Good Friday, the day that Christ was crucified. He died on Holy Saturday, the day before Easter. That Sunday, Easter, he was deified in many churches, especially in the North, as a god-like "Savior." Newspapers picked up on this theme and the mythical Lincoln was born.

Some, who knew him well, wanted people to know Lincoln as a real man, not a saint-like caricature. His long-time friend and third, and final, law partner, William (Billy) Herndon, researched Lincoln's early years, contacting people who knew him and exploring written material he found. He began lecturing about Lincoln and with the help of another writer published:

- *Herndon's Lincoln* (1889)

  ⊳ Herndon's lectures and this book were largely based on anecdotal and oral histories. Such source material is difficult to verify and might be subject to exaggeration and distortion. Lincoln's romance with Ann Rutledge, a friend who died young, may be an example. Her relatives stressed the depth of this romance to Herndon and he shared this view in lectures years before his book was published (he was no fan of Mary Lincoln, nor she of him). Mary Lincoln and her son Robert were outraged (she was incensed) with the stories. Later scholars questioned the accuracy of some of these anecdotes. Lincoln's friendship with Ann Rutledge was certainly real and he mourned her early death with great sorrow. But Lincoln was typically very ill at ease around young women, while quite comfortable with older women in whose homes he frequently boarded. But because Ann was officially engaged to a man who had gone East to settle some personal business, one author suggests that Lincoln felt comfortable with her but not necessarily in a romantic way.

- *The Life of Lincoln, from his Birth to his Inauguration as President* (1872), by Ward Lamon

- *Recollections of Abraham Lincoln* (1895) by Ward Lamon et al.

Perhaps the first book, published only seven years after Lincoln's death, was by Ward Lamon (Lincoln's long-time friend and unofficial bodyguard), and was based on some of Herndon's research,

EARLY BOOKS

- *Works of Abraham Lincoln's* (1890) by Nicolay and Hay (10 volumes)

  ⏵ Lincoln brought his two main secretaries, John Nicolay and John Hay, to Washington from Illinois with him. They lived in the Executive Mansion. Robert Lincoln, who had possession of many of his father's papers, provided access to them for their books. Robert then gave the papers to the Library of Congress with the condition that they not be opened until 21 years after his own death. Robert, Lincoln's only surviving son, died July 26, 1926.

- *Inside the White House in War Times* (1890), by William Stoddard

> ▷ A third secretary, William Stoddard, was hired to handle the voluminous mail that came into the White House. This experience caused Stoddard to later write, "I am convinced that when a person goes insane in this country the first thing he does is write a letter to the president."

- *The Early Life of Abraham Lincoln* (1896) by Ida Tarbell

- *The Life of Abraham Lincoln* (1900) by Ida Tarbell

- *In the Footsteps of the Lincolns* (1924) by Ida Tarbell

> ▷ Tarbell was an investigative reporter, a "muckraker," who took on John D. Rockefeller and Standard Oil, and won.

- *Abraham Lincoln: The Prairie Years* (1926) (2 volumes), by Carl Sandburg

- *Abraham Lincoln: The War Years* (1939) (4 volumes), by Carl Sandburg.

> ▷ Carl Sandburg was a noted American poet who won a Pulitzer Prize for his Lincoln books.

LATER WRITERS

Writers in the early and middle 1900s tended to take a more scholarly approach to research, often dismissing the oral histories of the past. More recently, however, the early oral histories seem to be coming back into favor.

Many writers seem to see Lincoln from a very personal perspective:

- *Lincoln's Melancholy: How Depression Challenged A President and Fueled His Greatness* (2005) by Joshua Wolf Shenk

  ▷ This author suffered from depression, as did Lincoln, in his opinion. Lincoln certainly did have two very low emotional periods.

- *The Physical Lincoln* (2008) by John G. Sotos, MD

  ▷ This author concludes that Lincoln suffered from a rare genetic disorder called MEN2B. His mother and three of his sons died young, and the author thinks Lincoln would have been dead within a year if he hadn't been assassinated.

- *The Intimate World of Abraham Lincoln* (2005) by C.A. Tripp

  ▷ This author makes the case that Lincoln was homosexual. Scholars are critical of the research, and have disagreed with its conclusion.

- *Lincoln's Sanctuary – Abraham Lincoln and the Soldier's Home* (2003) by Matthew Pinsker

  ▷ In the hot and humid District of Columbia summers the Lincoln family escaped the sweltering White House by moving to higher ground four or five miles away, to a cottage on the grounds of the Soldiers' Home. Lincoln would commute to his office in the Executive Mansion each day. This home was restored and opened to the public in 2008.

- *Mr. Lincoln's T-Mails* (2006) by Tom Wheeler

  ▷ The author tells us that the first really modern war was won by a leader who loved technology, and masterfully used the relatively new telegraph to communicate with his army and share news with the country

- *Killing Lincoln* (2011) by Bill O'Reilly and Martin Dugard

  ▷ A well-researched book on the Booth conspiracy – one that ended in the murder of our 16th president.

- *Lincoln: The Biography of a Writer* (2008) by Fred Kaplan

  ▷ The author claims that Lincoln's words were shaped through early exposure to Shakespeare, the King James Bible, Aesop's Fables, the writings/speeches of Thomas Jefferson, John Bunyan, Henry Clay, and classical writers, and poets such as Thomas Gray and Oliver Wendell Holmes and others. Still he wrote to the people. As another European writer declared, in his opinion the first two great "American" writers were Lincoln and Mark Twain.

- Lincoln – An Illustrated Biography (1992) by Kunhardt et al.

  ▷ This book provides accurate text and a remarkably full photographic record of Lincoln's adult life.

EXCELLENT MORE RECENT BOOKS

- *Lincoln at Gettysburg: The Words That Remade America* (1993) by Garry Wills

  ▷ The great political writer Garry Wills won a Pulitzer Prize for this volume that elucidates how Lincoln wrote the Gettysburg Address.

- *Lincoln* (1995) by David Herbert Donald

  ▷ Donald's biography is generally thought of as one of the very best single-volume biographies of Lincoln.

- *Battle Cry of Freedom: The Civil War Era* (2003) by James M. McPherson

  ▷ An excellent book focusing on how Lincoln handled the crises of the Civil War, including military, political, and social conditions.

- *Lincoln at Cooper Union: The Speech That Made Abraham Lincoln President* (2005) by Harold Holzer

  ▷ In this book, Holzer analyzes Lincoln's 1860 speech, stating that the speech was not only responsible for making Lincoln the leading Republican presidential candidate for president but also that the speech outlined the policies that were the basis for his election.

- *Team of Rivals: The Political Genius of Abraham Lincoln* (2006) by Doris Kearns Goodwin

  ▷ Goodwin's book details Lincoln's dual facilities for interpreting people's characters and setting up relationships. This history delves deeply into the backgrounds of Lincoln's cabinet members. In addition, it describes how Lincoln managed to create a winning team from such dissimilar individuals. (Steven Spielberg, as noted earlier, used *Team of Rivals* as the historical basis for his film *Lincoln*.)

- *Tried by War: Abraham Lincoln as Commander in Chief* (2008) by James McPherson

  ▷ McPherson contends that Lincoln did not violate individuals' civil liberties as much as later presidents who were facing less critical circumstances. McPherson focuses also on how perceptive and talented a war leader he was, indeed, that he apparently had a stronger grasp of military strategy than some Civil War generals, especially McClellan.

- *Emancipating Lincoln – The Proclamation in Text, Context, and Memory* (2012) by Harold Holzer

> ▷ In this relatively slim volume, Holzer details how Lincoln, once he was convinced that freeing the slaves was important both economically and morally, excruciatingly rewrote the Emancipation Proclamation three times. He argues that it did not make a difference that the document accomplished little at that particular time, that it indeed set up the extinction of the institution of slavery in the United States.

- *Lincoln and the World* (2013) by Kevin Peraino

  > ▷ Focusing on a series of episodes involving foreign policy, Peraino details Lincoln's good judgment and patience in dealing with foreign leaders and issues. In his opinion Lincoln often proved "more adept at the arts of diplomacy than the polished and gold-braided envoys of Europe."

- *Becoming Lincoln* (2018) by William W. Freehling

  > ▷ Provides an interesting review of how Lincoln grew as a person, with a strong case that much of his development was in response to not wanting to be his father. The author goes into even more detail about Lincoln's political development.

- *Lincoln's Confidant* (2019) by Wayne C. Temple

  > ▷ We learn about Noah Brooks, an influential journalist who became Lincoln's close friend and confidant

during Lincoln's presidency. Brooks also became close to Mary Lincoln, and wrote about seeing a very happy Lincoln on the last day of his life.

AN ENLIGHTENED STATESMAN, OR A RACIST DESPOT?

Lincoln mania has also allowed Lincoln haters to flourish. Two book examples of this phenomenon are *Forced into Glory* (2000) and *The Real Lincoln* (2002).

Detractors of Lincoln claim he was a racist, dictator, and butcher, and support these claims with charges to which I will respond.

∞

Charge – he made racist comments on the inequality of the races.

Response – When running for the senate in Illinois against Stephen Douglas he said some very offensive things. Illinois was not a slave state but it also was not black friendly. During their seven debates Douglas would say, "This man wants to free the slaves, who will then come here to take your daughters and your jobs." While Lincoln did say that the races weren't necessarily equal, he never deviated from arguing that they were equal in the right to eat the bread they earned. He basically left a lucrative law practice and got back into politics because of his hatred for the Fugitive Slave Act and the Dred Scott Supreme Court decision saying slaves had no rights.

Charge – that Lincoln really fought the war more over preserving the Union rather than over the issue of slavery.

Response – This is true. He felt the federal government did not have the right to end slavery, that it was up to each state to end it as many states had already done. He was insistent, however, that it not be allowed in the new states being formed from western territories. But once the war had started he knew that slavery had to end, and he worked hard on getting the thirteenth amendment passed, which would end slavery forever.

Charge – that the Emancipation Proclamation was limited to the slaves in the eleven Confederate warring states and not to the five slave-holding border states, which had not joined the Confederacy (Delaware, Maryland, Kentucky, Missouri, and West Virginia, the last having "seceded" from Virginia after Virginia had seceded from the Union). As Lincoln famously said, "I hope to have God on my side but I absolutely need Kentucky."

Response – This is true; it was an executive order issued in wartime to discourage England and France from recognizing the Confederate nation. They needed cotton for their textile factories and the blockade was preventing this. Once this Proclamation was announced, slavery, not independence, became the main issue and these other countries backed off. Lincoln well knew the limitations of the Emancipation Proclamation and was working behind the scenes with Congress to get the 13th Amendment passed, which would end slavery forever. He lived to see it passed but not to see it ratified.

[An interesting footnote to the signing of the Emancipation Proclamation.

Lincoln was determined to sign the document on January 1, 1863. New Year's Day at the White House was traditionally an afternoon open house, and the president would stand for hours shaking hands with long lines of eager citizens.

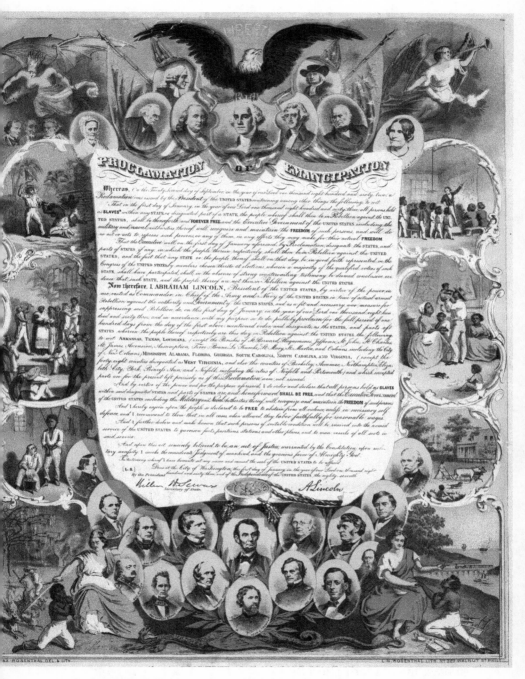

Emancipation Proclamation. Courtesy of Library of Congress.

119

Early in the morning the long document had been dictated, rushed to the State Department to be formally transcribed, then returned for Lincoln's signature. Lincoln signed, as did his Secretary of State, William Seward. But then Lincoln saw a mistake in the document itself. It read: "In testimony where of I have hereunto set my name and cause the seal of the United States to be affixed." This was the language used to proclaim treaties that had been ratified by Congress. The Emancipation Proclamation was Lincoln's own executive order; the correct phrase should be, "In witness where of I have hereunto set my hand..." He ordered the document re-written – to be signed later that day.

That afternoon, after shaking hands for hours, his hands were trembling, causing him to remark that he hoped people seeing his scrawled signature wouldn't infer that he was nervous about signing it. He declared "I never, in my life, felt more certain that I was doing right, than I do in signing this paper...if my name ever goes into history it will be for this."

This signed, flawed copy of the Emancipation Proclamation is part of an extensive Lincoln collection, including one of the five copies of the Gettysburg Address in his handwriting, at Cornell University.]

Charge – that he was a supporter of colonization of the freed slaves, away from the US.

Response – Lincoln was a realist. He saw problems with former slaves living next door to and going to school with former owners, especially in states with very large slave populations. In the early 1800s colonization was put forth by Daniel Webster, Francis Scott Key, Henry Clay, and other enlightened leaders as a humane opportunity for freed slaves. The African country of Liberia (liberty) was actually created by freed black slaves. Lincoln brought this up as an option several times, but when told by a group of black leaders that they had no interest in this, saying their families had been in this country for much longer than many of the more recent immigrants, Lincoln dropped the idea and never pushed it again.

∞

Charge – that during the war he assumed illegal powers, including suspension of Habeas Corpus (right to a fair and speedy trial) on occasion.

Response – He did use force to ensure that Maryland, a slave state, not join the Confederacy. Washington, DC, was surrounded by slave states, and Virginia had already seceded. He could not allow Maryland to do the same. He asked, why should I observe all the laws of the constitution while southerners, and northern "copperheads" were breaking them and encouraging Union soldiers to desert? He occasionally shut down newspapers and jailed or exiled some agitators.

But he never hesitated about holding a national

presidential election in 1864, an election he felt strongly, at least initially, that he would lose. What kind of dictator would do that? It wasn't until Sherman took Atlanta that the anti-war sentiment in the north began to shift. Lincoln ended up winning that election with 55% of the popular vote.

⁓

Charge – that he got us into a needless war, responsible for more deaths than all other wars combined.

Response – He did not want a war; he made that clear in his first Inaugural Address. But once it was started by the Confederate forces who fired on Fort Sumter, he knew he had to win it decisively to bring the warring states (he never considered them an independent country) back into the Union fold. He wanted healing, not vengeance. This attitude shaped Grant's terms when Robert E. Lee surrendered. America was whole again.

⁓

Summary – These negative authors/pundits do not attempt to put these events or words into context and explain when or why they were done or said. Nor do they acknowledge any evolution and growth of Lincoln himself. Finally, and worst of all, these so-called "historians" use very selective research, employing negative "facts" when useful to their point of view, but ignoring balancing or contrary information.

Without a Lincoln this country would not be the country it is today.

[Regarding Lincoln and race. As an attorney he was involved in at least three cases dealing with race.

- In 1841, he won a court case (*Bailey v. Cromwell*), representing a black woman and her children, who claimed she had already been freed and could not be sold as a slave.

- In 1845, he successfully defended Marvin Pond (*People v. Pond*) for harboring a fugitive slave.

- In 1847, he lost a case (*Matson v. Rutherford*) representing a slave owner (Robert Matson) claiming return of fugitive slaves.

- It is this last case, the fact that once he represented a slave owner, along with some of his statements about the social inequality of the races, that has occasionally fractured the once solid African-American admiration for Lincoln.

During his administration he helped end slavery in the District of Columbia. Black leaders like Frederick Douglass and Sojourner Truth became supporters, Douglass rather belatedly. He initially felt Lincoln was moving too slowly on using black troops in the war, and in ending slavery. But to most of the black population in both the north and the south, he was a messiah. When the Confederate capital, Richmond, was captured, Lincoln, his son, and a small military contingent walked its streets. Whites stayed indoors sullenly staring, but blacks filled the streets, some getting onto their knees before "Father Abraham." This embarrassed him, and he kept repeating, "Get up! Don't kneel to any man, only to God."

This admiration for Lincoln by the black population was the norm for the next century. It culminated in 1963 when civil rights leader Martin Luther King, Jr., delivered his famous "I Have a Dream" speech in Washington, DC. Opening it with, "Five score years ago, a great American, in whose symbolic shadow we stand today, signed the Emancipation Proclamation..." Almost immediately these remarks received heated responses. Militant civil rights activist Malcolm X declared that King was a fool, using Lincoln's own quotes and facts such as his defending a slave owner, to "prove" that Lincoln was a racist. Others echoed this, including white supremacists who jeered, "He didn't like you any more than we do."

For the next four decades it was fashionable for blacks, if they mentioned Lincoln at all, to do it in a disparaging way. An editor of *Ebony* magazine wrote a book saying that he grew up in the south adoring Lincoln until he learned the "truth," repeating what Lincoln said about social equality, that he defended a slave owner, and that the Emancipation Declaration really didn't free any slaves, etc., etc. I actually heard this man give that talk to a large university audience. At another public gathering I heard a young black, hip hop executive deliver a similar message.

In 2009 this attitude changed again. Barack Obama, a young black politician from Illinois, decided to run for the presidency. He used the Illinois connection with Lincoln as a key part of his campaign. He kicked off his campaign in front of the old Illinois State Capitol building, as Lincoln did, citing Lincoln a number of times in his talk. He took the train to Washington to be sworn in, as did Lincoln. And he was sworn into office on a Lincoln family bible, twice. Lincoln was acceptable again.

Lincoln is now generally recognized as one of the best friends that Americans, both white and black, have ever had. This includes many southern whites, who now concede that the reconstruction era, and the bitterness it caused for almost a century, might have been completely different if Lincoln had lived.]

LINCOLN LORE #43

PRESIDENT LAFAYETTE SABINE FOSTER, OR MAYBE, SCHUYLER COLFAX

Once John Wilkes Booth decided to assassinate Lincoln, he planned to wipe out the leadership of the Union government. When he learned that the president and his wife would be attending *Our American Cousin* at Ford's Theatre he decided to act. He had also heard that General Grant and his wife would be accompanying the Lincolns and planned to kill Grant too, but that day found out that the Grants had left Washington for New Jersey. Undeterred, he instructed his co-conspirators, Lewis Powell and George Atzerodt, to simultaneously slay Secretary of State William Seward and Vice President Andrew Johnson. Powell was to kill Seward, who was in bed in his home because of a carriage accident, and Atzerodt would kill Andrew Johnson at his hotel in Washington.

Booth was successful in killing the president, but Powell only wounded Seward. Atzerodt didn't even attempt to carry out his assignment.

What would have happened if Booth had succeeded in killing the president, the vice president, and the Secretary of State? According to the laws of succession in effect at that time, in the absence of a president and vice president an Acting President would be appointed until a special election would be held. (That election would be for a president, not a vice president.) The appointed Acting President would be the president pro-tempore of the Senate, who was Senator Lafayette Sabine Foster of Connecticut. If he had not been available it would have been Speaker of the House Schuyler Colfax, from Indiana (who later would actually become Vice President under President Grant in 1869).

Clarification of presidential succession, and questions of competence to serve, were addressed by the 20th and 25th Amendments.

As for the conspirators, Booth was slain after a long chase through Maryland and northern Virginia. Lewis Powell, George Atzerodt, and two others, David Herold, and Mary Surratt, were found guilty by a Military Tribunal, and hanged.

THAT REMINDS ME OF A STORY...

Lincoln is quickly recognized by his top hat, his beard, and his penchant for telling stories. He developed this into an art form and seemed to have an unlimited supply of stories to use as needed. Many may have been acquired during his years of traveling on the Eighth Legal Circuit, swapping stories and humorous anecdotes with his fellow gypsy lawyers.

Not everyone particularly liked his storytelling, suggesting it lowered the status of the executive office and was "unbecoming." But what really mattered was that Lincoln found it useful in many different ways, and continued to use them when he thought appropriate.

What critics did not comprehend, but what Lincoln's friends well understood, is that storytelling was at the core of the president's character. "The habit of story-telling," recalled Hugh McCulloch, who was named Secretary of the Treasury in March 1865, "became part of his nature and he gave free rein to it, even when the fate of the nation seemed to be trembling in the balance. ... Story-telling was to him a safety-valve, and that he indulged in it, not only for the pleasure it afforded him, but for a temporary relief from oppressing cares; that the habit had been so cultivated that he could make a story illustrate a sentiment and give point to an argument."

His humor drew people to him and made him likable. Lincoln shrewdly used stories and parables in more complex ways as well. They would disarm opponents, or offer an easily digestible truism that seemed to support whatever position he might be taking.

According to Lincoln himself, "You speak of Lincoln stories. I don't think that is a correct phrase. I don't make the stories mine by telling them. I'm only a retail dealer." And, "There are two ways of relating a story. If you have an auditor [listener] who has the time, and is inclined to listen, lengthen it out, pour it out slowly as if from a jug. If you have a poor listener, hasten it, shorten it, shoot it out of a pop-gun."

To a critical delegation from New York, which tried to embarrass him by asking for a "story," he replied, "I believe I have the popular reputation of being a story-teller, but I do not deserve the name in its general sense, for it is not the story itself, but its purpose or effect that interests me. I often avoid a long and useless discussion by others, or a laborious explanation on my own part, by a short story that illustrates my point of view. So, too, the sharpness of a refusal or the edge of a rebuke may be blunted by an appropriate story so as to save wounded feelings and yet serve the purpose. No, I am not simply a story-teller, but story-telling as an emollient saves me much friction and distress." The humbled delegation left the White House with a new respect for their president.

A contemporary said, "Mr. Lincoln wasn't a storyteller in the sense that people tell stories for the thing in the story. I doubt if he ever told a story just because it was a story. If he told an anecdote it was to illustrate, or make more clearly, some point he wanted to impress. He had a marvelous aptitude for that..."

Anyone who met with him commented on his endless supply of anecdotes and jokes. Count Adam Gurowski, a Polish exile who worked in the State Department, observed, "In the midst of the most stirring and exciting – nay, death-giving – news, Mr. Lincoln has always a story to tell." Ralph Waldo Emerson found it delightful: "When he has made his remark, he looks up at you with a great satisfaction, shows all his white teeth, and laughs." Walt Whitman thought it was "a weapon which he employed with great skill."

A few examples:

Abraham Lincoln was often criticized, by the media and others. One day, after Lincoln had read some particularly scathing articles, his secretary John Hay recalled him telling this story: "A frontiersman lost his way in an uninhabited region on a dark and tempestuous night. The rain fell in torrents, accompanied by terrible thunder and more terrific lightning. To increase his trouble his horse halted, being exhausted with fatigue and fright. Presently a bolt of lightning struck a neighboring tree, and the crash brought the man to his knees. He was not an expert in prayer, but his appeal was short and to the point. 'Oh, good Lord, if it is all the same to you, give us a little more light, and a little less noise.'"

In response to being asked why he didn't react more angrily at being regularly criticized by a political opponent: "I feel about that a good deal as a man whom I once knew, did about his wife. He was one of your meek men, and had the reputation of being badly henpecked. At last, one day his wife was seen chasing him out of the house striking him with a switch. A day or two afterward, a friend of his met him on the street, and said: 'Jones, I have always stood up for you, as you know, but I'm not going to do it any longer. Any man who will stand quietly and take a switching from his wife deserves to be horse-whipped.' Jones looked up with a wink, patting his friend on the back. 'Now, don't,' he said. 'Why, it didn't hurt me any; and you've no idea what a power of good it did Sarah Ann!'"

Listening to two groups of men that came to argue as to whether or not a St. Louis church should be closed as a result of statements of disloyalty from its minister, Lincoln said that the situation reminded him of a story. He said that a man in Sangamon County had a melon patch that kept getting ruined by a wild hog. Finally he and his sons decided to take their guns and track the animal down. They followed the tracks to the neighboring creek, where they disappeared. They discovered them on the opposite bank, and waded through. They kept on the trail a couple of hundred yards, when the tracks again went into the creek, and promptly turned up on the other side. Having lost both his breath and his patience, the farmer said, "John, you cross over and go up on that side of the creek, and I'll keep up on this side, because I believe that hog is on both sides of the creek!" "Gentlemen," Lincoln said, "that is just where I stand in regard to your controversies in St. Louis. I am on both sides. I can't allow my generals to run the churches, and I can't allow your ministers to preach rebellion."

Another favorite Lincoln story was of the preacher who said, during his sermon, that although the Lord was the only perfect man, the Bible never mentioned a perfect woman. A woman in the rear of the congregation called out, "I know a perfect woman, and I've heard of her every day for the last six years." "Who was she?" asked the surprised minister. "My husband's first wife," came the reply.

One polished writer used Lincoln's dialect in sharing his response to a discussion about the pressure from abolitionists for the president to take action against slavery: Lincoln said, "Wa-al that reminds me of a party of Methodist parsons that was travelling in Illinois when I was a boy, and had a branch to cross that was pretty bad – ugly to cross, ye know, because the waters was up. And they got considerin' and discussin' how they should git across it, and they talked about it for two hours, and one on 'em thought they had ought to cross one way when they got there, and another another way, and they got quarrellin' about it, till at last an old brother put in, and he says, says he, 'Brethren, this here talk ain't no use. I never cross a river until I come to it.'"

LINCOLN LORE #45

A NATURAL ATHLETE

The doctors who tended Lincoln as he was dying from John Wilkes Booth's bullet were amazed at his muscular frame. They were seeing what many others knew. Lincoln was very strong, and one of the best athletes in any community in which he lived. He had worked at manual labor since he was a boy, behind a plow or chopping wood, and had developed tremendous strength. His long legs helped make him a very fast runner, and his long arms helped him in competitive sports in many ways. On top of that he never smoked or used tobacco in any form. Team sports really didn't exist but competitive tests of speed or of strength were common, and he enjoyed participating, and winning.

As a publication of that time wrote about Lincoln:

"It is scarcely necessary to add that he also greatly excelled in all those homely feats of strength, agility, and endurance practiced by frontier people in his sphere of life. In wrestling, jumping, running, throwing the maul and pitching the crow-bar, he always stood first among those of his own age."

Wrestling has been a popular sport since the beginning of our country, and Lincoln became adept at it. Most have heard of his wrestling match when he first arrived in New Salem, Illinois. A group of local rowdies, the Clary's Grove boys, would welcome male newcomers with a rough hazing or initiation to see "what the new man was made of." His boss, Denton Offutt, the owner of the store where he clerked, had seen young Lincoln lift barrels and perform other feats of strength, which absolutely amazed him. He began bragging about how strong Lincoln was to some of the young men frequenting his store. Of course it didn't take long for them to test this tall and lanky newcomer.

Jack Armstrong was the unofficial leader of this "gang," and considered the strongest man in the county. A challenge was made and accepted, and a match between Armstrong and Lincoln was scheduled. There are a number of versions of the outcome, so it is not entirely certain who won. A common theme is that during the spirited match Armstrong got frustrated with Lincoln's long arms and cheated in some way. Lincoln became furious and picked up Armstrong and threw him to the ground. What is certain is that Lincoln gained the admiration of Jack Armstrong and all the Clary's Grove boys, who became ardent supporters and friends. [Some of these men were part of the reason Lincoln was elected Captain of his militia company during the Black Hawk War. They helped in later political campaigns too. Years later he successfully defended the widow Armstrong's son in a famous murder trial.]

Some say that Lincoln wrestled at least 300 times, only losing once. During the Black Hawk War Captain Lincoln's militia company challenged another company to a match. Lincoln lost that match.

Once, while Lincoln was giving a speech, a fight broke out in the audience. He saw that a supporter of his was on the losing end. He jumped off the stage, grabbed the aggressor, and threw him a distance, then returned to the platform to finish his talk.

During his years as a lawyer in Springfield he played handball against the building walls in the alley next to his office. Occasionally there was a small money purse at stake to make the game interesting.

As president he loved visiting the troops in the field and he would often bond with them by suggesting that they produce their strongest fellow soldier and they would have a contest. Often they would use an axe to test for strength. Each would hold the axe in their outstretched arms as long as they could. Lincoln won enough times to deeply impress the much younger soldiers.

In 1992 the National Wrestling Hall of Fame inducted Abraham Lincoln.

LINCOLN LORE #48

PATRON OF THE ARTS

In one scene in the 1970s TV mini-series *Sandburg's Lincoln*, Hal Holbrook, as Lincoln, is waiting with some fellow lawyers in a tavern next to the courthouse in which the jury of his court case is deliberating. A woman enters saying she needs a lawyer. She introduces herself and says that she heads up a Shakespeare troupe but they can't perform until they buy a city council license, and she can't pay the fee until they sell tickets and perform. Lincoln stands and says, "Ma'am, if I am to convince them, then you have to convince me," and then dramatically recites:

> *We will proceed no further in this business.*
> *He hath honored me of late, and I have bought*

Golden opinions from all sorts of people,
Which would be worn now in their newest gloss,
Not cast aside so soon...

The woman responds, equally dramatically:

Was the hope drunk,
Wherein you dress'd yourself? Hath it slept since?
And wakes it now, to look so green and pale
At what it did so freely? From this time
Such I account thy love...

There is further exchange, and then Lincoln asks:

If we should fail?

She responds:

We fail!
But screw your courage to the sticking-place and we'll not fail.

At that point someone opens the door and loudly announces that the jury is back and they are to return to the courtroom. Lincoln dramatically departs, enthusiastically declaring, "I won't fail you, ma'am, I'll get your license."

It is wonderful bit of film "theater," and the dialogue from *Macbeth* is very appropriate. As Lincoln once wrote to an actor:

"For one of my age, I have seen very little of the drama... Some of Shakespeare's plays I have never read; while others

I have gone over perhaps as frequently as any unprofessional reader. Among the latter are Lear, Richard Third, Henry Eighth, Hamlet, and especially Macbeth. I think nothing equals Macbeth. It is wonderful. Unlike you gentlemen of the profession, I think the soliloquy in Hamlet commencing, 'O, my offence is rank' surpasses that commencing, 'To be, or not to be.' But pardon this small attempt at criticism."

We all knew Lincoln loved to read – but he also loved the theater, whether serious plays, comic productions, or musical productions of all kinds.

He couldn't play an instrument or carry a tune, but he passionately loved music. While in the White House he attended many operas, but also invited performers to entertain there, really starting what has now become a musical tradition. Mrs. Lincoln ordered a magnificent grand piano for the Red Room, and it became the center of entertainment.

Music could move him emotionally, creating both highs and lows. Friends observed that certain songs would mist his eyes and throw him into a fit of melancholy. "Listening to melody," he once said, "every man becomes his own poet, and measures the depths of his own nature, though he is apt to lose the line as the sound dies away."

The *New York Herald* suggested the Lincolns visit Manhattan, where Mary could shop, and he could have his fill of opera.

Some criticized his attending the theater while the war was ongoing. His response, "The truth is I must have a change of some sort, or die."

He liked the opera *Martha*, by Friedrich von Flotow,

and had it performed during the festivities for his second inaugural. One month before he died Lincoln attended a performance of Mozart's *Magic Flute* at the National Theatre in Washington. Lincoln first heard the song "Dixie" in Chicago before he became president. He considered it one of his favorite songs, even after it had become the unofficial national anthem of the southern Confederacy. At the gathering on the White House lawn, after Lee's surrender, he asked the musicians there to play "Dixie," saying, "Now it belongs to all of us." He also, of course, loved the "Battle Hymn of the Republic" and enjoyed greeting its composer, Julia Ward Howe, at a White House reception.

One musical group has been part of White House entertainment since John and Abigail Adams first moved in. The Marine Corps Band played at the Adams's New Year's party. From Jefferson's time the Marine Corps Band became known as "The President's Own." It would perform at special events, and also held concerts on the White House lawn. On July 25, 1861, President Lincoln officially recognized, by law, the role of the Marine Corps Band. [Antonio Sousa, father of John Phillip Sousa, was a member of the Marine Corps Band during Lincoln's administration. When he was thirteen, John Phillip Sousa, a gifted musician, planned to join a traveling circus as a musician. His father did not want that to happen and arranged to get young Sousa into the Marine Corps Band. He remained until he was twenty, and would go on to become the world-renowned "March King."]

HE WOULD HAVE WON THE ANIMAL VOTE TOO

Lincoln's instinctive empathy with animals came early. As a boy he would protest against those who hurt or tortured animals. When he discovered other boys hurting turtles in various ways, from putting them on their backs so they had trouble turning over, to much crueler treatment, he would forcibly stop them and lecture them about how wrong it was.

His stepmother reportedly said, "He loved animals, he loved children as well. Even insects, saying 'an ant's life is as sweet as ours.'" As a boy a pig became his pet and followed him around like a pet dog. When the pig attained the proper size his father slaughtered him to feed the family. Young

Lincoln was appalled, and would not eat any of that particular dish.

An early anecdote tells of him finding young birds on the ground and taking the time to find their nest and returning them. Another relates to his having passed a pig that was stuck in a mud hole. After walking on he felt bad and returned to free the pig, getting filthy in the process. A friend said it was because Lincoln would feel bad if he had just passed by. When his father moved the family from Indiana to Illinois, he decided to leave their family dog behind. At one river crossing the dog, who was following them, was in danger of drowning. Lincoln jumped into the river and saved the dog, saying to his father that, except for his own wet and cold feet, both he and the dog felt better now.

As has earlier been said, he wouldn't hunt. That was very unusual for a young man of that time. [For that matter, so was the fact that he didn't smoke or chew tobacco, curse, drink hard liquor (as an adult he might take an occasional wine, or hard cider), and called water his "Adam's Ale." But he had a rougher side too. He loved telling ribald stories to his men friends, and could use what today would be considered very "politically incorrect" language. And, as a young man, he participated in some crude practical jokes against other young men.]

He loved cats and dogs, and had both in his Springfield home and the White House. It is reported that when his wife was asked if Lincoln had any hobbies, she replied, "cats." His Springfield home had, besides the mandatory horse (his last three were Tom, Belle, and Old Bob), a cow for milk. He left his horse, Old Bob, and his yellow mongrel dog, Fido, behind with friends when he left for Washington. Jip became his Executive Mansion dog. He loved his cat Tabby, and two goats, Nanny and Nanko, as much as his boys did. He also is credited with beginning the tradition of "pardoning" their planned turkey dinner at Thanksgiving (apparently he actually pardoned his first turkey at Christmas time).

In 1863 the barn behind the White House was destroyed by a blazing fire, killing at least six horses – including a couple ponies belonging to his boys. He had to be forcibly restrained from entering the barn to fight the fire and try to save the horses. He wept openly.

After his funeral train finally arrived back in Springfield, the funeral parade to his burial ground included Old Bob, walking with an empty saddle and boots pointed backwards to signify the departed president/rider.

TILL DEATH DO US PART

Lincoln used to joke that his wife's family name, Todd, required two Ds, while God could get by with just one D. The fact is that even before he met Mary Todd, who eventually became his wife and mother of his four sons, a member of the extended Todd family played a major role in his life (which included introducing him to Mary).

John Todd Stuart was born in 1807 in Lexington, Kentucky. He became a lawyer and opened a practice in Springfield, Illinois. When the Black Hawk War broke out he served as a major in the same militia battalion in which Lincoln was a captain. They became good friends and later served in the state legislature together (both were Whigs). At one legislative session, which met in Vandalia before the state capital had moved to Springfield, they even shared a bed [a common practice in that era of limited, almost primitive, accommodations]. At the time Lincoln, while a member of the Legislature, was also working as a surveyor, but had few other options. Stuart saw his potential and suggested he study law. Lincoln well knew his educational shortcomings and was reluctant to even consider it. But Stuart was persistent, and working with him, he helped Lincoln become a practicing lawyer, and a junior partner in Stuart's law firm. [Ironically, when Lincoln was President, Stuart was a Democratic member of Congress and actually voted against the 13th Amendment, which passed and ended slavery forever.]

One of Stuart's favorite cousins was Mary Todd from Lexington, Kentucky. He ultimately helped Lincoln and Mary meet, and because she had heard so many stories from him about his unusual friend, she was eager to meet him.

Mary was the daughter of Robert Todd, a very successful businessman and a political activist. She was the fourth of seven children when her mother died. Her father remarried and nine more children were born. As one can imagine, she felt neglected and worked very hard at getting her father's attention and respect. She had the finest education, including good schools and then attendance at a local elite French boarding school. She would go home on weekends but during the week boarded at the school. She had the equivalent of a college degree, and could speak French fluently, which was very unusual for that time, especially for a woman. Her father was heavily involved in politics, as a Whig. The biggest names in national or state politics enjoyed dinners at the Todd mansion, and Mary would thrive on the discussions that took place. The celebrated Henry Clay lived nearby and was charmed by young Mary.

When Abraham and Mary finally met, the fact that they could both discuss classical literature in depth, as well as current politics, bonded them almost from the beginning. She, a well-educated young woman, he, an autodidact (self-taught). The fact that she had actually spent time with his political hero, Henry Clay, greatly impressed him.

Their courtship was mostly enjoyable for both of them, but had its rocky moments. He broke it off at one point and they didn't see each other for a long while. He went through a long melancholic period, sharing his concerns in letters to his good friend, Joshua Speed, who had recently gotten married. The fact that Speed was happy helped allay some of Lincoln's fears. Friends got them back together and her sister planned a big, social wedding. But Lincoln suddenly announced that they were going to get married the next day. After a small wedding in her sister's home, they went to live at the modest Globe Hotel for four dollars a week. Robert was born less than a year later. They moved to a one-story home, which her father helped them purchase. Ten years later they added a second floor. The home is currently open to the public.

She had grown up with servants but adapted remarkably quickly to the cooking, cleaning, sewing, and work demands of a young wife and mother in a rustic home. They had four boys, and she was a loving mother. There were some, occasionally public, disputes, but basically they were close, and she liked being Lincoln's confidante and counselor. She had a dread of thunderstorms, and if he was in town when one occurred he was very solicitous. However she was very unhappy with the amount of time that he would spend away from Springfield, on political or legal work. But in general theirs was a good, loving partnership. She had great pride and confidence in her "tall Kentuckian," and was less surprised than he was at his growing reputation and popularity. They sincerely liked each other and enjoyed spending time together.

Her time with him changed after his election to the presidency. Now he had many other counselors and advisors. And the press could be very cruel. He was a "country bumpkin," so of course she had to be one too. The fact that she came from the South and that many of her "kin" had joined the Confederacy didn't help. As was the custom of the time, they each had their own bedrooms in their Springfield home, and the Executive Mansion. But she saw much less of him in DC.

She really never recovered from losing her eleven-year-old son in the White House. Then after her husband was shot, and she held the dying man in her arms, she was never the same. She and her youngest son, Tad, escaped to Europe for a while but he died a few years later and she came back to the States. At one point her bizarre behavior caused Robert, her only surviving son, to have her committed to a mental hospital. She was released in a few months, but never really forgave Robert. She revisited Europe but returned to Springfield, becoming a recluse in her sister's house, where she had been married forty years before. She died in 1882, at sixty-three, wearing her wedding ring inscribed "Love is Eternal," and was buried next to her husband and three sons in Oak Ridge Cemetery in Springfield.

Mary Todd Lincoln might be one of the most misunderstood women in American political history.

HOW A VETO FROM A MEDIOCRE U.S. PRESIDENT HELPED CREATE THE "FIRST AMERICAN UNIVERSITY"

As discussed in Lincoln Lore #16, Lincoln's signing the Morrill Land Grant Act led to the creation of Cornell University. But as is so often the case, the actual details are much more complicated.

It can be said that Cornell was "The First American University." From the beginning it was to be coeducational, nonsectarian, and a Land Grant Institution; it was designed to have a broad-based curriculum and a diverse student body. These were relatively unheard of ideas at the time.

In the late 1850s Senator Justin Morrill of Vermont envisioned adding Agriculture and Engineering to the Humanities and Arts education of the time. [This was not an entirely new idea. The Agricultural College of the State of Michigan (now Michigan State University) was founded in 1855.] In 1859 Morrill's Land Grant Act was passed, allowing the federal government to give federal land to the states to be sold, with the proceeds used to create schools of Agriculture and Engineering. The bill was sent to the President, and our 15th president vetoed it. James Buchanan is generally considered to be one of the nation's worst presidents. This veto could be considered no big deal, since the Land Grant Act was resubmitted to President Lincoln in 1862 (with an added clause, that Military Science would be added to the curriculum), and signed by him.

The fact is: Buchanan's veto was a very big deal. If he had signed the bill instead of vetoing it, Cornell University would never have seen the light of day. New York State would have had a land grant college, of course, but it wouldn't have been Cornell.

Two extraordinary and very different men were elected to the New York State Senate in 1864. Andrew D. White was a young intellectual, educated at Yale, with a vision of a different and better university. Ezra Cornell was an older man with little formal education but a deep belief that education should be available to everyone, and should be very broad-based. He was basically a farmer with a strong technical bent, and thanks to his work with the relatively new telegraph system, he had become extremely wealthy. As state legislators, White and Cornell merged their dreams and ended up creating a unique educational institution with money from Land Grant funds and generous support from Cornell. Cornell's farm in Ithaca, New York, became the campus of the new university, and Andrew D. White its first president. Chartered in 1865, it opened in 1868 with the largest freshman class in U.S. history to date, 412 students.

Cornell honored Morrill by putting his name on its first new building built on campus. Lincoln was honored with his building in 1881. Ezra Cornell and Andrew D. White are well honored too, of course. But maybe Cornell needs a Buchanan Hall (perhaps its waste disposal area). As we now know, without his veto Cornell University would never have been born.

[Cornell also passed on some of its magic. In the 1880s Leland Stanford, who came from central New York State, wanted to build a world-class university in California. He invited Andrew D. White to be Stanford University's first president. White declined, but did recommend a Cornell graduate, David Starr Jordan. Jordan became Stanford's first president, and many of the initial faculty members were Cornell classmates of Jordan. Stanford was called the "Cornell of the West" when it opened.]

[Brown College, founded in 1764, now an Ivy League

University, was for a brief time the land grant college of the state of Rhode Island. Rhode Island's land grant designation was later switched from Brown to the Rhode Island State College, now known as the University of Rhode Island.]

"CARING FOR HIM WHO SHALL HAVE BORNE THE BATTLE..."

The horrors of the war tore at Lincoln's very soul. Washington, DC, became, in effect, one big hospital. There were so many wounded that almost all public buildings became hospitals, including at least thirty-six official hospitals. Lincoln would visit the wounded whenever he could.

One of the lesser-known stories of this time is how much time Mary also devoted to visiting the hospitals. She would bring flowers, candy, or anything else that she thought would be useful. While under great stress herself, and horrified by some of the wounds, she would read letters from home, and write letters from them to their loved ones. She tried to keep her visits private, but they would occasionally be written up in the press, usually in very short articles. Negative articles about her so-called "extravagances" or "thoughtless socializing" got much more space in the papers.

Here are a few personal accounts of Lincoln hospital visits:

"Weather clear and pleasant," wrote one patient. "Old Abe passed through on a 'shake hands' with all the patients."

Another wrote, "Uncle Abe gave us each a word of cheer."

For many of those standing outside the tents, the president's words were a simple "How do you do." Some of those unable to stand heard him say, "I hope you will soon be able to go to your friends." One, who had lost his leg below the knee recalled: "When he reached my bed he said: 'What, a leg gone?' I said: 'Yes.' He then took my hand in both of his. I asked him: 'Well, Father Abraham, have we done our work well.' He said: 'Very well indeed, and I thank you.' I never shall forget the pressure he gave my hand, nor can I forget that sad, careworn face." Fifty years later, recollecting that day, the soldier wrote: "I often see that sad and worn face in memory, and I can hardly keep back the tears."

"He had the manner of a gentleman—I may say of a gentle gentleman," wrote an agent for the U.S. Christian Commission; "his voice as we heard it was subdued and kindly; his eyes were mild but all-observing; and his face that he once himself described as 'poor, lean and lank,' was a strong face marked with lines of a mingled gentleness and sadness that redeemed it from being homely. The close grasp of his hand attested the sympathetic great heartedness of the great man."

A soldier with a shoulder wound remembered the Lincoln mantra, "Be of good cheer, boys; we are at the beginning of the end at last." To another he said that "the war will soon be over and then we'll all go home."

In one tent with twelve wounded officers was a Confederate Major who had fallen at the same time as the Union men. According to one Union man, Lincoln "gave this officer a hearty grasp of the hand and inquired what State he was from and where he resided before entering the Army. He then wished him a speedy and hasty recovery from his wounds, and told him that in a few days the war would be over and he would be able to see his dear ones at home." After Lincoln left, the dazed Rebel asked who the man was who had spoken to him and was stunned by the answer. "My God, is that so?" he exclaimed. "Is that the kind of a man that we have been fighting for four long years?"

There was another Confederate officer in a different tent he visited. That officer later recalled: "The president walked down the long aisle between the rows of cots on each hand, bowing and smiling. Arriving at length opposite where I lay, he halted beside my bed and held out his hand. Looking him in the face, as he stood with extended hand: 'Mr. President,' I said, 'do you know to whom you offer your hand?' 'I do not,' he replied. 'Well,' I said, 'you offer it to a Confederate colonel, who has fought you as hard as he could for four years.' 'Well,' said he, 'I hope a Confederate colonel will not refuse me his hand.' 'No, sir,' I replied, 'I will not,' and I clasped his hand in both of mine. I tell you, sir, he had the most magnificent face and eyes that I have ever gazed into. He had me whipped from the time he first opened his mouth."

On one visit, doctors directed Lincoln to a young soldier who was approaching death. The President went over to his bedside, asking, "Is there anything I can do for you?" The emaciated soldier clearly didn't know the man standing in front of him was President Lincoln. Not recognizing him, the wounded young man whispered to the President with some difficulty, "Would you please write a letter to my mother?" Lincoln duly complied and carefully jotted down what the soldier said on a piece of paper. "My dearest mother, I was badly hurt while doing my duty. I'm afraid I'm not going to recover. Don't grieve too much for me, please. Kiss Mary and John for me. May God bless you and father." The soldier stopped, as he was too frail to continue. Lincoln signed the letter, writing, "Written for your son by Abraham Lincoln." When the soldier saw the note Lincoln had written on his behalf, he was astonished to see Abraham Lincoln's signature at the end. "Are you really the President?" the young man asked. Lincoln replied, "Yes, I am" before asking if there was anything else he could do to assist him. In response, the soldier asked: "Would you please hold my hand? It will help to see me through to the end." In the quiet room, the tall, gaunt president held the young man's hand and offered him words of encouragement until he breathed his last.

A Vermont soldier recalled years afterward that Lincoln's

"tall form and loving face bent over every one of us. Not one did he pass by. And to every one he had some word of good cheer tenderly spoken, while his homely face became absolutely beautiful as it beamed with love and sympathy. He would say to each, 'God bless you, my boy! Keep up a good heart. You'll come through all right. We'll never forget you!'"

Just days before Lee surrendered, Lincoln visited Grant at his headquarters at City Point, Virginia. Nearby was one of the largest military hospitals in the country, housing thousands of patients. Lincoln was determined to visit the hospital and to shake the hand of every wounded soldier there. Officials kept trying to show him the facilities, kitchens, etc., of which they were very proud. He assured them that he was sure they had done an excellent job on setting the facility up, but that he was there to shake the hands of the men who had won the war for the Union. At the end of the day his arm ached painfully, "worse than a day of chopping wood or behind a plow." But he had achieved his goal – he had shaken every wounded soldier's hand.

SOLOMON-LIKE STATESMAN, SHREWD POLITICIAN — OR BOTH?

Politics – "The art or science of guiding or influencing governmental policy."
Statesman – "A wise, skillful, and respected political leader."

Lincoln was an idealist, somewhat of a dreamer. He wanted, more than anything else, to be respected by his fellow man. But he recognized early that one couldn't become a "statesman" without first being elected. Winning an election was everything. He honed his intuitive skills and became a political force to be reckoned with – a force that would "take no prisoners" when it came to achieving a political goal. He was a formidable political opponent.

From the very beginning he practiced what today would be called "retail politics." He loved meeting people, sharing stories, and learning what their needs and wants were. Yarn- and story-telling became an art form. It bought time and, if necessary, could help change the topic, help make subtle points, and change the tone of the discussion.

He would do favors for others, and wasn't bashful about asking for favors in return. As mentioned in Lincoln Lore #10, he only lost one popular-vote election. It was his first political foray, running for the State Legislature when he was twenty-three. Because of the Black Hawk War he could not campaign, and lost although still winning in his home dis- trict by a large margin.

He used his talent as a communicator, sending letters and guest editorials to newspapers throughout his political life. He could forget sleights, hold no grudges, and build connections and coalitions, whenever possible. One extremely supportive group of young men called themselves "Wide Awakes." They became very active and helped him get a rousing welcome wherever he appeared,

Then, as now, politicians did not always play by the rules. The 1860 Republican Convention was held in a huge, tempo- rary, wooden conference hall in Chicago called the Wigwam. Lincoln's friend Judge David Davis directed his campaign there, while Lincoln remained in Springfield. Besides Lincoln (Illinois), other serious candidates were William Seward (New York), Simon Cameron (Pennsylvania), Edward Bates (Missouri), and Salmon Chase (Ohio); in total, there were thirteen potential candidates. Delegates were given passes to gain entrance to the Center. Davis had counterfeit passes printed, distributed them to men with the loudest voices he could find, and got them to the Wigwam early. Whenever Lincoln's name was mentioned. the building rocked with the cheers from the Lincoln delegation. Lincoln clinched the nomination on the third ballot.

In both presidential campaigns Lincoln used basic Politics 101 to "balance the ticket." Hannibal Hamlin of Maine was the VP candidate for Lincoln, the Western candidate, in 1860. In 1864 he selected Andrew Johnson, a pro-war Democrat from Tennessee, as his running mate.

There were four candidates in the 1860 election: Lincoln, Republican; John C. Breckinridge, Southern Democrat; Stephen A. Douglas, Northern Democrat; and John Bell, Constitutional Party. While gaining less than 40% of the popular vote, Lincoln overwhelmingly won the Electoral College vote.

In the 1864 election Lincoln ran as the candidate of the National Union Party, against George McClellan, Democrat. [McClellan had once been Lincoln's boss. As president of a railroad in Illinois he had hired Lincoln as one of its lawyers.] As a general under Lincoln, McClellan had organized and trained an impressive army. His troops loved him. But he was an ineffective war general, refusing to fight. Lincoln fired him twice, replacing him with a fighting general, Grant.

Although the Union soldiers were fond of McClellan, they adored Lincoln and played a pivotal role in his reelection. Many states had passed laws permitting absentee ballot voting, though some Democratic states did not. Knowing the feelings of the soldiers, commanders allowed them to take home leave during the voting time. While capturing 55% of the popular vote, Lincoln won 78% of the military vote, becoming the first president to be reelected since Andrew Jackson in 1832.

As an elected official Lincoln demonstrated a good sense of timing. Several of his generals had issued slave emancipation orders in the areas they occupied. Lincoln was not pleased. He felt that while the soldiers from Maine or Wisconsin would fight and die for the Union, he wasn't sure they were willing to die for the black man down in Mississippi. He ordered these generals to rescind their orders. Then on January 1, 1863, he issued his own Emancipation Proclamation, which also authorized the use of black men in the military. They eventually made up to 10% of the Union Army.

As the war began to obviously wind down, both sides desperately wanted a peace agreement. Lincoln wanted it too, but he knew that a precondition on the part of the Confederacy would be the restoration of legal slavery in the south. Lincoln encouraged peace talks but used all manner of delays to avoid a decisive sit-down until the slavery issue was resolved.

As Mark Twain famously said, "Those who like sausage and respect the law should watch neither being made." This would be especially appropriate as Lincoln twisted arms in Congress to get the 13th Amendment passed, ending slavery forever; "horse trading" when possible, playing "hardball" when necessary, he pulled out all stops. It was finally passed on January 31, 1865. Peace would come, but slavery was gone.

[This successful but difficult and "messy" political effort was brilliantly captured in the 2012 movie *Lincoln*, directed by Steven Spielberg.]

GEORGE AND ABRAHAM, TWO TOWERING PRESIDENTS

Since 1948 there have been at least 20 scholarly surveys ranking our presidents. The average results rank Lincoln #1, Franklin Delano Roosevelt (FDR) #2, and George Washington #3.

In my opinion FDR was an extraordinary war president, guiding this country, actually the entire free world, through World War II against the evil and formidable Axis powers of Germany, Japan, and Italy. However, again in my opinion, his first seven years in office are more problematic. Regardless, he was the only president elected to four terms. Now each president is limited to two terms.

I am confident that Mr. Lincoln would agree with me that Washington was certainly our greatest president, and deserves the #1 ranking. He really created our country, and literally defined what our presidency could and should be.

Then, I submit, should come President Lincoln, the leader who preserved the Union, as #2. Without him I am convinced that the America we know would be a Balkanized series of smaller nations extending from the east coast to the west coast. I will leave it to others to suggest what presidents should follow, and in what order.

Lincoln truly admired George Washington and considered him a model, in both his personal and political life. As a young boy he learned the cost of learning when he borrowed a book on Washington from a neighbor. After reading it he went to sleep in his cabin's loft bed, stowing the book in the attic eaves. A heavy rain damaged the book and Lincoln gave three days' labor to the farmer to pay for it. But he now owned a slightly damaged but readable book of his hero. When he left Springfield for Washington, to be sworn in as president, he gave tribute to Washington in his farewell remarks. And on that trip he happened to be in Philadelphia on February 22, Washington's birthday. He gave a short talk in Independence Hall, among other things paying tribute to Washington.

Washington and Lincoln had a number of things in common besides serving as our first and our sixteenth president respectively. They were both tall (Washington 6'2", Lincoln 6'4"), they were both very good wrestlers; neither had much formal education, Washington had some tutoring, but like Lincoln, was primarily self taught; both had been surveyors (Washington quite extensively, Lincoln much less so); both farmers (Washington a plantation owner, Lincoln a laborer); both served in the militia (Washington as its senior officer, Lincoln briefly as a Captain); both declared days of national Thanksgiving (Washington in 1789 and 1795, Lincoln as an annual holiday in 1863); both were elected to a second term; both were awarded honorary doctoral degrees (Washington from Harvard; Lincoln from Knox, Columbia, and Princeton); both are on our currency, stamps, and Mount Rushmore; both have February birthdays (Washington February 22, Lincoln February 12); both have impressive memorials in DC; and, most importantly, both were prolific wordsmiths, leaving a marvelous "paper trail" for historians to follow.These include diaries, journals, speeches, letters, articles, and interviews.

[One odd tribute they share is that both men were honored with statues showing them half clothed. A statue showing a standing "Young Lincoln," with no shirt, one hand on his waistband and the other holding a book, is at the Federal Courthouse in Los Angeles. A statue showing a seated Washington, with only a sheet draped over one arm and covering his lower body, sits like a Roman emperor in the National Museum of Natural History, Smithsonian Institution, DC.]

Lincoln had offered Robert E. Lee, a former Superintendent at West Point, an opportunity to head the U.S. Army. Lee considered it but when his state, Virginia, seceded from the Union, Lee felt obligated to join them. Lee's father,

Henry Lee III, a general under Washington, had famously praised our first president at Washington's funeral, declaring him, "First in war, first in peace, and first in the hearts of his countrymen." Robert E. Lee, who had surrendered his army about a week before Lincoln was assassinated, deplored Booth's action, calling it a "crime."

[America's annual "Presidents' Day" holiday has had an interesting history. It is held on the third Monday in February. It all began in 1800, after Washington's death in 1799. February 22, his birthday, became a widespread but unofficial day of celebration. In 1885 "Washington's Birthday," February 22, became a federal holiday. In the 1960s it was shifted to the third Monday to provide a regular three-day holiday. And its name was changed to Presidents' Day so that Abraham Lincoln's February 12 birthday might also be included. (Presidents William Henry Harrison and Ronald Reagan were also born in February, but they don't seem to be mentioned on Presidents' Day.)]

QUOTABLE GEMS

If any personal description of me is thought desirable, it may be said I am, in height, six feet four inches, nearly; lean in flesh, weighing, on an average, one hundred and eighty pounds; dark complexion, with coarse black hair, and grey eyes – no other marks or brands recollected.

I don't know who my grandfather was; I am more concerned to know what his grandson will be.

My early life is characterized in a single line of Gray's Elegy: "The short and simple annals of the poor."

History is not history unless it is the truth.

In the end, it's not the years in your life that count. It's the life in your years.

All that I am, or hope to be, I owe to my angel mother. I remember her prayers, and they have always followed me. They have clung to me all my life.

The lady bearer of this says she has two sons who want to work. See them if at all possible. Wanting to work is so rare a want that it should be encouraged.

I was not much accustomed to flattery and it came the sweeter to me. I was rather like the Hoosier with the gingerbread, when he said he reckoned he loved it better than any other man, and got less of it.

You must remember that some things legally right are not morally right.

With educated people, I suppose punctuation is a matter of rule; with me it is a matter of feeling. But I must say I have a great respect for the semi-colon, it is a useful little chap.

I don't think much of a man who is not wiser today than he was yesterday.

Others have been made fools of by the girls, but this can never with truth be said of me. I most emphatically, in this instance, made a fool of myself.

I have now come to the conclusion never again to think of

marrying, and for this reason – I can never be satisfied with anyone who would be blockhead enough to have me.

I want in all cases to do right, and most particularly so in all cases with women.

It is difficult to make a man miserable when he feels worthy of himself, and claims kindred to the great God who made him.

I have endured a great deal of ridicule without much malice; and have received a great deal of kindness, not quite free of ridicule.

Nearly all men can stand adversity, but if you want to test a man's character, give him power.

I have always found that mercy bears richer fruit than strict justice.

We can complain because rose bushes have thorns, or rejoice because thorn bushes have roses.

I claim not to have controlled events, but confess plainly that events have controlled me.

If I were to try to read, much less answer, all the attacks made on me, this shop might as well be closed for other business. I do the very best I know how – the very best I can; and I mean to keep doing so until the end. If the end brings me out all right, what is said against me won't amount to anything. If the end brings me out wrong, ten thousand angels swearing I was right would make no difference.

As for being president, I feel like the man who was tarred and feathered and ridden out of town on a rail. To the man who asked how he liked, it he said, "If it wasn't for the honor of the thing, I would rather walk."

I am not accustomed to the use of the language of eulogy; I have never studied the art of paying compliments to women; but I must say, that if all that has been said by orators and poets since the creation of the world in praise of women were applied to the women of America, it would not do them justice for their conduct during this war. I will close by saying, God bless the women of America!

CLASSIC POETIC TRIBUTES

How three poets remembered and honored Lincoln.

The first, "Nancy Hanks," was first published in a *Book of Americans* in 1933. In 1941 music was added and it became a song. During that period many schoolchildren learned to recite or sing the song.

The second, "O Captain! My Captain!," is a moving tribute to Lincoln and how he successfully sailed the ship of state through a storm of war, only to be killed before landing. It became very popular.

And finally, Paul Laurence Dunbar, who wrote "Lincoln," was born in 1872 in Dayton, Ohio. His parents had been slaves in Kentucky. He died young, at 33, but had great recognition as a gifted writer.

"NANCY HANKS"
BY ROSEMARY BENET

If Nancy Hanks came back as a ghost,
Seeking news of what she loved most,

She'd ask first "Where's my son?
What's happened to Abe? What's he done?

Poor little Abe, left all alone
Except for Tom, who's a rolling stone;

He was only nine the year I died.
I remember still how hard he cried.

Scraping along in a little shack,
With hardly a shirt to cover his back,

And a prairie wind to blow him down,
Or pinching times if he went to town.

You wouldn't know about my son?
Did he grow tall? Did he have fun?

Did he learn to read? Did he get to town?
Do you know his name? Did he get on?"

"O CAPTAIN! MY CAPTAIN!" BY WALT WHITMAN

O Captain! my Captain! Our fearful trip is done,

The ship has weather'd every rack, the prize we sought is won,

The port is near, the bells I hear, the people all exulting,

While follow eyes the steady keel, the vessel grim and daring;

    But O heart! heart! heart!

      O the bleeding drops of red,

        Where on the deck my Captain lies,

        Fallen cold and dead.

O Captain! my Captain! Rise up and hear the bells;

Rise up—for you the flag is flung—for you the bugle trills,

For you bouquets and ribbon'd wreaths—for you the shores

    a-crowding,

For you they call, the swaying mass, their eager faces turning;

    Here Captain! dear father!

      This arm beneath your head!

        It is some dream that on the deck,

        You've fallen cold and dead.

My Captain does not answer, his lips are pale and still,

My father does not feel my arm, he has no pulse nor will,

The ship is anchor'd safe and sound, its voyage closed and done,

From fearful trip the victor ship comes in with object won;

    Exult O shores, and ring O bells!

      But I with mournful tread,

        Walk the deck my Captain lies,

        Fallen cold and dead.

"LINCOLN"
BY PAUL LAURENCE DUNBAR

Hurt was the nation with a mighty wound,
And all her ways were filled with clam'rous sound.

Wailed loud the South with unremitting grief,
And wept the North that could not find relief.

Then madness joined its harshest tone to strife:
A minor note swelled in the song of life.

'Till, stirring with the love that filled his breast,
But still, unflinching at the right's behest,

Grave Lincoln came, strong handed, from afar,
The mighty Homer of the lyre of war.

'Twas he who bade the raging tempest cease,
Wrenched from his harp the harmony of peace,

Muted the strings, that made the discord,—Wrong,
And gave his spirit up in thund'rous song.

Oh mighty Master of the mighty lyre,
Earth heard and trembled at thy strains of fire:

Earth learned of thee what Heav'n already knew,
And wrote thee down among her treasured few.

II

LINCOLN, ORATOR EXTRAORDINAIRE

Lincoln became obsessed with being able to communicate properly. From his youth until his later life he drove himself to master the ability to communicate, not only ideas but also feelings, to others through the written or the spoken word.

As a boy in Indiana he would practice speaking in the woods, sometimes standing on a tree stump. He would talk to an imaginary audience or maybe the neighborhood children. Occasionally he would mimic a sermon they had heard, eliciting laughter from the children. He learned early the value of humor in communicating with an audience. As a young man he became part of several debating societies and learned the importance of research, preparation, and practice in delivering a message. He would never deliver an impromptu speech if at all possible. His gift with words as a writer served him well as an orator. One renowned speechwriter of the mid-1900s said that undoubtedly the finest presidential speechwriter in American history was Abraham Lincoln, who of course wrote his own speeches.

This section will briefly examine nine important Lincoln speeches. He delivered hundreds of them but these nine are memorable for a number of reasons. They include his first campaign speech; the "House Divided" speech; seven debates with Douglas; the Cooper Union speech, which put him on the national political map; his farewell to friends on leaving Springfield for Washington; his first Inaugural speech; the iconic Gettysburg Address; his second Inaugural speech; and lastly, his final speech, delivered just three days before he was assassinated.

Background and Excerpts of:
    (1) First political campaign speech
    (2) "House Divided" speech
    (3) Lincoln-Douglas debates
    (4) Cooper Union speech
    (5) Farewell to Springfield speech
    (6) First Inaugural speech
    (7) Gettysburg Address
    (8) Second Inaugural speech
    (9) Final speech from White House window three days before assassination

1

FIRST POLITICAL SPEECH GIVEN AT PAPPSVILLE, ILLINOIS, 1832

His first political campaign speech, running for a seat in the State Legislature, was given at Pappsville, Illinois, in 1832. He was 23 years old. He had also submitted an article to the *Sangamo Journal*. The article concluded with, "Every man is said to have his peculiar ambition...I have no other so great as that of being truly esteemed of my fellow men, by rendering myself worthy of their esteem."

After announcing his campaign he joined the militia because of the Black Hawk War. Because he couldn't actively campaign he lost this election. Two years later he ran again and won, ending up serving four consecutive terms in the Illinois Legislature.

> Fellow Citizens – I presume you all know who I am. I am humble Abraham Lincoln. I have been solicited by many friends to become a candidate for the legislature. My politics are short and sweet, like the old woman's dance. I am in favor of a National bank. I am in favor of the internal improvement system and a high protective tariff. These are my sentiments and political principles. If elected I shall be thankful; if not, it will be all the same.

2

"HOUSE DIVIDED" SPEECH, JUNE 16, 1858

More than 1,000 delegates met in the Springfield, Illinois, Statehouse for the Republican State Convention. They chose Abraham Lincoln as their candidate for the U.S. Senate, running against incumbent Democrat Stephen A. Douglas. Lincoln delivered this address. The title reflects part of the speech's introduction, "A house divided against itself cannot stand," a biblical statement. Some say the speech was so controversial that it cost him the Senate election, but all agree that it gave him national recognition.

Under the operation of that policy [putting an end to slavery agitation], that agitation has not only, *not ceased*, but has *constantly augmented.*

In *my* opinion, it *will* not cease, until a *crisis* shall have been reached, and passed.

"A house divided against itself cannot stand."

I believe this government cannot endure, permanently half *slave* and half *free.*

I do not expect the Union to be *dissolved* – I do not expect the house to *fall* – but I *do* expect it will cease to be divided.

It will become *all* one thing or *all* the other.

3

LINCOLN-DOUGLAS DEBATES IN 1858

Democrat Stephen A. Douglas, a well-known political figure, was running for his third term as senator. Lincoln, a relative unknown, was the candidate of the new Republican Party. Douglas delivered well-attended speeches in Chicago and Springfield. Lincoln "stalked" Douglas, delivering rebuttal speeches a day or two later at each location. The press, and Lincoln, urged more formal debates, and Douglas finally agreed to seven debates around the state of Illinois (Ottawa, Freeport, Jonesboro, Charleston, Galesburg, Quincy, and Alton). Each would be three hours long, with Douglas opening four of them, and Lincoln, three. The opening speaker would speak for an hour, the other speaker would respond for an hour and a half, and then the first speaker would have a half-hour to rebut and wrap up. These debates were published and widely read. They helped make Lincoln a national figure, though he lost the election. At that time the state legislatures selected their federal senators. Lincoln won the most votes in the state election, but the Democrat majority in the Legislature, as the electors, selected Douglas as the Illinois senator.

In the northern towns where the debates were held, Lincoln's stand on slavery was much more supported by the attendees. But in the more southern Illinois debate towns, those nearer to slave-holding states, attendees were closer to Douglas's stand on the slavery issue. Douglas would tell the audience that Lincoln's freed slaves threatened their jobs and families. Lincoln responded that he didn't believe in racial social equality. Lincoln haters have used those words over the next century and a half to "prove" that Lincoln was a racist. They ignore the political context, a politician attempting to win votes in a non-black-friendly portion of a non-black-friendly state. They don't mention that Lincoln never deviated from his main theme, that in the right to eat the bread that one earns by his own sweat, the Negro was his equal and the equal of everyone there.

Douglas tended to repeat some of his points. Lincoln would introduce new thoughts but might repeat some of these lines in letters or other talks, and used humor adroitly. When they were in Galesburg a heavy storm forced the organizers to move the speakers' platform to the walls of the Knox College main building. To get to the stage the participants had to go out an upper floor window of the building down a ladder to the platform. Lincoln reportedly joked, "I can now say I have gone through college," never imagining, as he made this jest, that this Knox College would later be the first of three colleges to award him an honorary Doctor of Laws degree.

> I say upon this occasion I do not perceive that because the white man is to have the superior position the Negro should be denied everything.
>
> I confess myself as belonging to that class in the country who contemplated slavery as a moral, social and political evil
>
> ...these poor tongues of Judge Douglas and myself shall be silent. It is the eternal struggle between these two principles – right and wrong – throughout the world. They are the two principles that have stood face to face from the beginning of time; and will ever continue to struggle. The one is the common right of humanity, and the other the divine right of kings. It is the same principle in whatever shape it develops itself. It is the same spirit that says, "You toil and work and earn bread, and I'll eat it." No matter in what shape it comes, whether from the mouth of a king who seeks to bestride the people of his own nation and live by the fruit of their labor, or from one race of men as an apology for enslaving another race, it is the same tyrannical principle.

4

COOPER INSTITUTE (UNION), NEW YORK, FEBRUARY 27, 1860

Lincoln had been invited to speak at a church in Brooklyn by its pastor, Henry Ward Beecher. Some New York Republicans were looking for an alternate presidential candidate, feeling front runner William Seward, though highly successful and well known, was too controversial because of his strong stand against slavery. They knew Lincoln also opposed slavery but felt he was less militant. They were able to get the speech moved to a larger venue in lower Manhattan, the Cooper Union. Law partner Billy Herndon said that Lincoln worked harder than he ever had on a speech to present a highly researched indictment of slavery. [1500 people attended, paying $.25/person; he was paid $200 plus expenses]

After the speech Lincoln took a copy to the newspapers; he wanted an exact copy printed. On this trip he also went to famed photographer Mathew Brady for a full-length picture. Brady was able to make a man whose homely features were often mocked look presidential. Both photo and speech helped Lincoln get elected. While in the East he also received a number of invitations to speak. He turned down some in New Jersey but did speak in some New England cities, and was able to visit his son Robert, who was at Exeter Academy in New Hampshire, preparing to attend Harvard.

> Let us be diverted by none of those sophistical contrivances wherewith we are so industriously plied and belabored – contrivances such as groping for some middle ground between the right and the wrong, vain as the search for a man who should be neither a living man nor a dead man – such as a policy of "don't care" on a question about which all true men do....
>
> Neither let us be slandered from our duty by false accusations against us, nor frightened from it by menaces of destruction to the Government nor of dungeons to ourselves. LET US HAVE FAITH THAT RIGHT MAKES MIGHT, AND IN THAT FAITH, LET US, TO THE END, DARE TO DO OUR DUTY AS WE UNDERSTAND IT.

5

FAREWELL ADDRESS, SPRINGFIELD, ILLINOIS, FEBRUARY 11, 1861

Early on Monday, February 11, President-elect Lincoln, with his brand-new beard (he didn't have a beard when he was elected in November), headed to the train station to leave for Washington, DC. He stopped at his bank to withdraw $400 and deposit a check for $82.25 (from the sale of certain household goods). He was accompanied by his son, Robert. His wife Mary and the other two boys, Willie and Tad, were out of town and would join them in Indianapolis.

The next day would be his 52nd birthday. There were many friends and admirers at the station. He shook hands and gave a brief farewell talk. Observers said there were tears in his eyes. On the train he wrote down the remarks he had just delivered and gave them to the reporters on board. A journey that could have been made in a few days took almost two weeks because of frequent stops. Everyone along the way wanted to see the new president. Shortly after the trip had begun there was a moment of panic because the valise containing his inaugural speech was missing. It was soon found. While in Harrisburg, Pennsylvania, nearing the end of his journey, he was told of a credible threat to assassinate him as he changed trains in Baltimore, in the slave-holding and Southern-sympathizing state of Maryland. He and his associate, Ward Lamon, changed their clothing look and as inconspicuously as possible took a different train to DC, arriving there on Saturday, February 23.

> My friends, no one, not in my situation, can appreciate my feeling of sadness at this parting. To this place, and the kindness of these people, I owe everything. Here I have lived a quarter of a century, and have passed from a young to an old man. Here my children have been born, and one is buried. I now leave, not knowing when, or whether ever, I may return, with a task before me greater than that which rested upon Washington. Without the assistance of the Divine Being who ever attended him, I cannot succeed. With that assistance I

cannot fail. Trusting in Him who can go with me, and remain with you, and be everywhere for good, let us confidently hope that all will yet be well. To His care commending you, as I hope in your prayers you will commend me, I bid you an affectionate farewell.

FIRST INAUGURAL ADDRESS, MARCH 4, 1861

Lincoln wrote this speech while still in Springfield, after his election. He reviewed all previous inaugural talks and as usual worked extremely hard to develop his speech, one that hopefully would bring those states which had left the Union back and keep other states from joining them. While usually writing his own speeches, this time he did allow his Secretary of State, William Seward, to suggest a conciliatory addition. Lincoln's gift with words is evident when you compare Seward's final suggested sentence, "will yet harmonize in their ancient music when breathed upon by guardian angels of this nation," with Lincoln's final version, below.

...In *your* hands, my dissatisfied fellow-countrymen, and not in *mine,* is the momentous issue of civil war. The Government will not assail *you.* You can have no conflict without being yourselves the aggressors. *You* have no oath registered in heaven to destroy the Government, while I shall have the most solemn one to "preserve, protect, and defend it."

I am loath to close. We are not enemies, but friends. We must not be enemies. Though passion may have strained it must not break our bonds of affection. The mystic chords of memory, stretching from every battlefield and patriot grave to every living heart and hearthstone all over this broad land, will yet swell the chorus of the Union, when again touched, as surely they will be, by the better angels of our nature.

Abraham Lincoln's First Inauguration. Courtesy of Library of Congress.

7

GETTYSBURG ADDRESS, NOVEMBER 19, 1863

Lincoln was invited to say a few words at the dedication of the National Cemetery at Gettysburg, Pennsylvania, a few months after that bloody but pivotal battle. He would follow the main oration by Edward Everett, considered one of the greatest orators in the country. Everett would speak for two hours; Lincoln's speech lasted less than three minutes. For years it was said that Lincoln wrote his speech on the back of an envelope on the train from Washington. In fact, of course, Lincoln worked very hard on this speech, as he did on all of his talks, and polished it right up to the time it was delivered. It was well received, except by the partisan news-papers, which panned it, but wouldn't reach its iconic status for decades.

[Here is what three contemporary newspapers had to say about the Gettysburg Address:

The Chicago Times: "The cheek of every American must tingle with shame as he reads the silly flat and dish-wa-tery remarks of the man who has to be pointed out as the President of the Unites States...Is Mr. Lincoln less refined than a savage?...It was a perversion of history so flagrant that the most extended charity cannot view it as otherwise than willful?"

The London Times: "The ceremony was rendered ludi-crous by some of the sallies of the poor President. Anything more dull and commonplace it would not be easy to produce."

Harrisburg Patriot and Union: "The President succeeded on this occasion because he acted without sense and without constraint in a panorama that was gotten up more for the benefit of his party than for the glory of the nation and honor of the dead...we pass over the silly remarks of the President: for the credit of the nation we are willing that the veil of oblivion shall be dropped over them and they shall no more be repeated or thought of."

In 2013, 150 years later, the Harrisburg paper printed this apology, "Seven score and ten years ago, the forefathers of this media institution brought forth to its audience a judgment so flawed, so tainted by hubris, so lacking the perspective history would bring, that it cannot remain unaddressed in our archives...the Patriot & Union failed to recognize its momentous importance, timeless eloquence, and lasting significance. The Patriot-News regrets the error."]

Four score and seven years ago our fathers brought forth on this continent, a new nation, conceived in Liberty, and dedicated to the proposition that all men are created equal.

Now we are engaged in a great civil war, testing whether that nation, or any nation so conceived and dedicated, can long endure. We are met on a great battle-field of that war. We have come to dedicate a portion of that field, as a final resting place for those who here gave their lives that that nation might live. It is altogether fitting and proper that we should do this.

But, in a larger sense, we can not dedicate – we can not consecrate – we can not hallow – this ground. The brave men, living and dead, who struggled here, have consecrated it, far above our poor power to add or detract. The world will little note, nor long remember what we say here, but it can never forget what they did here. It is for us the living, rather, to be dedicated here to the unfinished work which they who fought here have thus far so nobly advanced. It is rather for us to be here dedicated to the great task remaining before us – that from these honored dead we take increased devotion to that cause for which they gave the last full measure of devotion – that we here highly resolve that these dead shall not have died in vain – that this nation, under God, shall have a new birth of freedom – and that government of the people, by the people, for the people, shall not perish from the earth.

8

SECOND INAUGURAL ADDRESS, MARCH 4, 1865

When Lincoln was sworn in for the second time it was clear that the South could not continue the fight. Lincoln was only concerned with bringing the seceded states back into the family of states, to heal the nation. It was an overcast day but during his speech the clouds parted and a ray of sunshine shone down. Many saw that as a message from God. That evening at the White House Reception he shook thousands of hands, including those of the first black man (Frederick Douglass) who attended such an event. When greeting him President Lincoln asked, "I saw you in the crowd today, listening to my inaugural address, how did you like it?" "Mr. Lincoln," Douglass responded, "that was a sacred effort." Many historians agree, saying that in spite of the poetic beauty of the Gettysburg Address, this almost sermon-like address was his finest speech.

...Both [North and South] read the same Bible and pray to the same God, and each invokes His aid against the other. It may seem strange that any men should dare to ask a just God's assistance in wringing their bread from the sweat of other men's faces, but let us judge not, that we be not judged. The prayers of both could not be answered. That of neither has been answered fully. The Almighty has His own purposes. "Woe unto the world because of offenses; for it must needs be that offenses come, but woe to that man by whom the offense cometh." If we shall suppose that American slavery is one of those offenses which, in the providence of God, must needs come, but which, having continued through His appointed time, He now wills to remove, and that He gives to both North and South this terrible war as the woe due to those by whom the offense came, shall we discern therein any departure from those divine attributes which the believers in a living God always ascribe to Him?...

...With malice toward none, with charity for all, with firmness in the right as God gives us to see the right, let us strive on to finish the work we are in, to bind up the nation's wounds, to care for him who shall have borne the battle and for his widow and his orphan, to do all which may achieve and cherish a just and lasting peace among ourselves and with all nations.

9

HIS FINAL SPEECH, APRIL 11, 1865

Lee surrendered on Sunday, April 9. Washington, DC, and the rest of the northern states erupted in joy. A torch-lit parade marched on the Executive Mansion for some remarks from the president. He came to the window to say to the crowd that he wasn't prepared, but to come back on Tuesday evening and he would speak to them.

His speech wasn't an eloquent oration; it was a business-like commentary on the challenges of bringing states like Louisiana back into the Union, and what its government should look like.

In the audience that Tuesday evening was John Wilkes Booth and a companion. At one point in the speech Lincoln mentioned that black men, especially those who fought for the Union, should get the franchise (i.e., be allowed to vote). Booth, who had been working with others on a plan to kidnap Lincoln to trade for Confederate soldiers being held in the North, was appalled and reportedly said to his associate, "That man has given his last speech." Three days later Booth shot Lincoln at Ford's Theatre.

> We meet this evening, not in sorrow, but in gladness of heart. The evacuation of Petersburg and Richmond, and the surrender of the principal insurgent army, give hope of a righteous and speedy peace whose joyous expression can not be restrained. In the midst of this, however, He, from Whom all blessings flow, must not be forgotten. A call for a national thanksgiving is being prepared, and will be duly promulgated. Nor must those whose harder part gives us the cause of rejoicing, be overlooked. Their honors must not be parcelled out with others. I myself, was near the front, and had the high pleasure of transmitting much of the good news to you; but no part of the honor, for plan or execution, is mine. To Gen. Grant, his skillful officers, and brave men, all belongs. The gallant Navy stood ready, but was not in reach to take active part.
>
> By these recent successes the re-inauguration of the national authority – reconstruction – which has

had a large share of thought from the first, is pressed much more closely upon our attention. It is fraught with great difficulty. Unlike the case of a war between independent nations, there is no authorized organ for us to treat with. No one man has authority to give up the rebellion for any other man. We simply must begin with, and mold from, disorganized and discordant elements. Nor is it a small additional embarrassment that we, the loyal people, differ among ourselves as to the mode, manner, and means of reconstruction...

III

LESSONS FROM
LINCOLN

CURIOSITY, CONVICTION, COURAGE, COMPASSION, COMMUNICATIONS, CHARACTER

Curiosity – Lincoln had no formal education. He taught himself to learn to read and write, and became an expert author and orator. He read for pleasure and for knowledge, he devoured books. But he had the same curiosity about people and events and studied them as assiduously as he studied books. He is, for instance, the only president to have patented an invention. He became an accomplished lawyer; no one has ever argued more cases before the Illinois Supreme Court than did Abraham Lincoln. As newspaperman Horace Greeley said, "He was open to all impressions and influenced and gladly profited by the teachings of events and circumstance, no matter how adverse or unwelcome. There was probably no year of his life when he was not a wiser, cooler, and better man than he had been the year preceding."

Conviction – Lincoln was nineteen when he first saw the true evils of slavery. He had helped float a flatboat down the Mississippi to New Orleans, where he witnessed a slave auction. He became an ardent opponent of slavery and never wavered from that position. He later said, "As I would not be a slave, so I shall not be a master..." and "Let us discard all this quibbling about this man and the other man – this race and that race and the other race...Let us discard all these things, and unite as one people throughout this land, until we shall once more stand up declaring that all men are created equal." This conviction culminated in 1863 when Lincoln began the end of slavery in America by signing the Emancipation Proclamation. Knowing this was a limited war measure he campaigned hard to end slavery by getting Congress to pass the 13th amendment. He lived long enough to see it passed, but did not live to see it ratified by the states a year later.

Courage – There are a number of examples of his physical courage, including his first journey to DC as president through the pro-South and slave State of Maryland, and his visit to Richmond, the capital of the Confederacy, soon after Lee's surrender, but I would rather focus on his moral courage. Lincoln was perhaps the most slandered, libeled, and hated man to ever run for the presidency. He was called a grotesque baboon, a third-rate country lawyer who once split rails and now splits the Union, a coarse vulgar joker, a dictator, an ape, a buffoon and worse. Nothing deterred him from his goal, although these experiences perhaps did make him more sensitive to the feelings of others. He never became bitter or vindictive. As he said, "Neither let us be slandered from our duty by false accusations against us, nor frightened from it by menaces of destruction to the government nor of dungeons to ourselves. Let us have faith that right makes might, and in that faith, let us, to the end dare to do our duty as we understand it."

Compassion – Lincoln knew sorrow. His beloved mother died when he was nine. His only sister died when he was nineteen. Of his four sons, Edward died at the age of three, Willie at eleven. But he also knew love. When he was ten his father remarried and his stepmother, Sarah, became very close to him. Both mothers loved him dearly and supported his hunger to learn. As a young man he shot a turkey and it convinced him that he didn't like hunting and never hunted again. Ironically, he led the country during one of the bloodiest wars in its history. During that war the Army was plagued with desertions, an offense punishable by death. Lincoln was criticized for pardoning so many deserters. In typical fashion he used humor to address this very serious issue, "If the Lord gives a man a pair of cowardly legs, how can he help their running away with him."

⸜∞⸝

Communications – He believed in the beauty and power of words, both written and spoken. He has been acclaimed as one of the finest writers this country has ever produced and gave some of the most memorable speeches in its history. Hard work and repetitive practice sharpened these skills. He would read whatever he could find and listened to conversations and talks with a critical ear. He wrote a great deal, starting when he was young, while also practicing oratory and debate.

⸜∞⸝

Character – Lincoln first earned the nickname "Honest Abe" as a young storekeeper known for being meticulously honest when dealing with customers. He was often asked to mediate disputes and contests. Later he famously repaid the debts of a failed business venture. A debt he could have walked away from, but over many years he paid off what he called the national debt. As a lawyer he advised other lawyers, "Resolve to be honest in all events…" His political rival, Stephen Douglas, said, "He is as honest as he is shrewd." There are many examples of him practicing what he preached, "Stand with anybody that stands right. Stand with him while he is right and part with him when he goes wrong." As one author who wrote about Lincoln's leadership qualities put it, "Lincoln would also become disdainful and enraged whenever dishonesty, in whatever form, reared its head...Even though he had some detractors, Lincoln attained success, admiration, and a positive image by maintaining his integrity and honesty. Those who questioned his upbringing and education, or even his political, affiliations, tended not to doubt his integrity."

IV

WORLDWIDE TRIBUTES TO LINCOLN

MEMORIALS

Memorials include Lincoln, Nebraska (1867). In 1867 when Nebraska became a state, a town called Lancaster was renamed Lincoln and became the state capital.

Following Lincoln's death, the first public monument was a statue erected in front of the DC City Hall in 1868.

The historic Lincoln Highway, the first road for cars to span the United States, represented the first national memorial to Abraham Lincoln. Running from New York City to San Francisco, it was dedicated in 1913.

In 1922 the Lincoln Memorial in Washington, DC, was dedicated.

Perhaps the oldest organization regularly honoring Lincoln is the Lincoln Association of Jersey City, New Jersey. Formed in 1865, they meet for a banquet every year on his birthday, February 12.

POSTAGE STAMPS

Only George Washington has appeared on more stamps in the USA. Lincoln is the only person depicted on an airmail stamp. In addition, he is pictured on foreign stamps more than any other American. Perhaps surprisingly, the very first foreign stamps honoring Abraham Lincoln were issued by the tiny Republic of San Marino in 1938. As the world's oldest constitutional republic, independent since the eleventh century, the republic had granted honorary citizenship to Lincoln on March 29, 1861. In his gracious acceptance of the honor, Lincoln noted, "Although your domain is small, your State is one of the most honored in all history."

TOWNS

PBS produced a map depicting cities and towns named after Abraham Lincoln. At that time, there were more than thirty. Perhaps unsurprisingly, no towns in the South were named for Abraham Lincoln. Counties or towns in the South named Lincoln were a tribute to Benjamin Lincoln, a Revolutionary War general.

SCHOOLS

A great many schools and colleges across the United States have Lincoln as part of their name, among them Lincoln University in Pennsylvania, California, and Missouri, and the University of Nebraska-Lincoln. In Illinois alone, 89 public schools include Lincoln as part of their name.

SOME AMERICAN STATUES

- bas relief on the "Michigan Soldiers' and Sailors' Monument," Detroit, Michigan, 1867

- *Abraham Lincoln*, Lot Flannery, Washington, DC (1868)

- *Abraham Lincoln*, Henry Kirke Brown, Union Square, New York City, NY (1870)

- *Abraham Lincoln*, Henry Kirke Brown, Prospect Park, Brooklyn, NY (1869)

- *Abraham Lincoln*, Vinnie Ream, United States Capitol rotunda, Washington, DC (1871)

- *Lincoln Tomb*, Larkin Goldsmith Mead, Springfield, Illinois (1874)

- *Emancipation Memorial*, Thomas Ball, Washington, DC (1876)

- *Abraham Lincoln: The Man*, aka *Standing Lincoln*, Augustus Saint-Gaudens, Chicago, Illinois (1887)

- *Abraham Lincoln Statue and Park*, Clermont, Iowa, 1902

- *Abraham Lincoln: The Head of State* aka *Seated Lincoln*, Augustus Saint-Gaudens, Chicago, Illinois (1908)

- *Abraham Lincoln*, Adolph Alexander Weinman, Hodgenville, Kentucky (1909); replica at University of Wisconsin, Madison (1909)

- *Seated Lincoln*, Gutzon Borglum, Newark, New Jersey (1911)

- *Abraham Lincoln*, Adolph Alexander Weinman, Kentucky State Capitol, Frankfort, Kentucky (1911)

- *Standing Lincoln*, Daniel Chester French, at the Nebraska State Capitol, Lincoln, Nebraska (1912)

- *Abraham Lincoln*, J. Otto Schweizer, at The Pennsylvania State Memorial, Gettysburg, Pennsylvania (1913)

- *Abraham Lincoln*, George Grey Barnard, Cincinnati, Ohio (1917)

- *Abraham Lincoln* in the Lincoln Memorial, Daniel Chester French (1914–22)

- *Abraham Lincoln*, Haig Patigian, Civic Center, San Francisco, California (1926)

- *Lincoln the Lawyer*, Lorado Taft, Urbana, Illinois, (1927)

- *Abraham Lincoln*, George Fite Waters, South Park Blocks, Portland, Oregon (1928)

- *Mount Rushmore*, Gutzon Borglum (1927–41)

- *Lincoln Monument*, Leonard Crunelle, Dixon, Illinois (1930)

- *Pioneer Backwoodsman, Preservation of the Union* and *Emancipation Proclamation* (three panels), Lincoln Bank Tower, Fort Wayne, Indiana, 1930

- *Emancipation Proclamation*, Lee Lawrie, Nebraska State Capitol, Lincoln, Nebraska, (1932)

- *Abraham Lincoln: The Hoosier Youth*, Paul Manship, Fort Wayne, Indiana, (1932)

- *Abraham Lincoln Walks at Midnight*, by Fred Torrey in 1933, cast by Bernard Wiepper, West Virginia State Capitol (1974)

- *Lincoln Trail State Memorial*, Nellie Verne Walker, near Lawrenceville, Illinois (1938)

- *Abraham Lincoln Monument*, Samuel Cashwan, Ypsilanti, Michigan (1938)

- *The Chicago Lincoln*, aka *Beardless Lincoln*, Avard Fairbanks, Chicago, Illinois (1956)

- *Young Abe Lincoln*, David K. Rubins, Indianapolis, Indiana (1962)

- *Young Abraham Lincoln*, also known as *Abraham Lincoln on Horseback*, *Abraham Lincoln Equestrian Monument*, and *Abraham Lincoln on the Prairie*, Anna Hyatt Huntington, editions located in Northwood Institute, Midland, Michigan (1963); State University of New York, College of Environmental Science and Forestry, Syracuse, New York (1963); Salem State Park, Petersburg, Illinois (1963–64); Lincoln City, Oregon (1965)

- Mr. Lincoln's Square, Clinton, Illinois

- Statue of Lincoln "outside the old ironworks that pow-
  ered the Confederate artillery," Richmond, Virginia

FOREIGN TRIBUTES

Admiration for Abraham Lincoln was not limited to the
United States:

"Great Russian Tells of Reverence for Lincoln Even
Among Barbarians," declared the headline of the *New York
World* newspaper on February 7, 1909.

Days before the Centennial of Lincoln's life in 1909, a
writer from the *New York World* newspaper visited the famous
Russian writer Leo Tolstoy to request an article on Lincoln.
Tolstoy was too ill to write an article but did agree to an
interview. Here is some of what he said:

> Of all the great national heroes and statesmen of
> history Lincoln is the only real giant. Alexander, Fred-
> erick the Great, Caesar, Napoleon, Gladstone and even
> Washington stand in greatness of character, in depth
> of feeling and in a certain moral power far behind Lin-
> coln. Lincoln was a man of whom a nation has a right
> to be proud; he was a Christ in miniature, a saint of
> humanity, whose name will live thousands of years in
> the legends of future generations. We are still too near
> to his greatness, and so can hardly appreciate his divine
> power; but after a few centuries more our posterity will

find him considerably bigger than we do. His genius is still too strong and too powerful for the common understanding, just as the sun is too hot when its light beams directly on us.

During Lincoln's lifetime he received praise from Karl Marx, the author of the *Communist Manifesto*. Exiled from Germany, Marx was living in London when he wrote of Lincoln in 1863, "...his most recent proclamation – the Emancipation Proclamation – [is] the most significant document in American history since the founding of the Union and one which tears up the old American Constitution." He later wrote a letter of congratulations to Lincoln on his reelection to the presidency.

Interest in Lincoln can be measured by the languages that tell his story. As is stated in *The Global Lincoln*, "By 1900, Lincoln's life had been published in (sequentially) German, French, Dutch, Italian, Portuguese, Greek, Spanish, Danish, Welsh, Latin, Hawaiian, Hebrew, Russian, Norwegian, Finnish, Turkish, Swedish and Japanese; and over the next thirty years or so the list had extended to include Ukrainian, Yiddish, Polish, Chinese, Tamil, Czech, Icelandic, Arabic, Hungarian, Persian, Slovak, Armenian, Scottish Gaelic, Korean, Kannada, Burmese and Vietnamese." These were, in most part, translations of texts originally written in English.

The first statue of Lincoln outside the United States, the work of George Edwin Bissell, was erected in Edinburgh, Scotland, in 1893. It stands on a memorial to Scots immigrants who enlisted with the Union during the Civil War and represents the only memorial to the war erected outside the United States.

A statue sculpted by George Grey Barnard was erected in Manchester, England, in 1919. It now stands in Lincoln Square west of Manchester Town Hall, Also in England, on July 28, 1920, a large statue of Lincoln standing, by Saint-Gaudens, was unveiled near Westminster Abbey in London.

A large bust of Lincoln was given to the people of Norway by the people of North Dakota in 1914 and installed in Vigeland Park in Oslo. When Lincoln signed the Homestead Act in1862, thousands of Norwegians were able to settle in the Dakotas. This bust is flanked by engraved bronze tablets, one excerpting the Gettysburg Address and the other inscribed: "Presented to Norway by the people of North Dakota, U.S.A., July 4th, 1914." During the World War II German occupation of Norway, thousands of Norwegians would gather at the statue on July 4th in silent prayer and protest at their lack of freedom

United States President Lyndon Johnson presented a Saint-Gaudens Lincoln statue to the people of Mexico, which is displayed in Mexico City's Parque Lincoln.

There is a likeness of Lincoln – the structure created by Henri Marquet and the mosaics done by Vincent Charra – that was dedicated at the University of Chicago Center in Paris, France, in honor of the first international conference on Lincoln, which was held at the Sorbonne in 2009.

V

THE LIFE OF ABRAHAM LINCOLN - A CHRONOLOGY

YEAR	AGE	EVENTS
1637		Samuel Lincoln emigrates from Hingham, England, and settles in Hingham, Massachusetts
1778		Thomas (Tom) Lincoln (Abraham's father), descendant of Samuel, is born in Virginia; Tom's father is named Abraham
1782		Grandfather Abraham and family, including Thomas, move to Kentucky (paid $88 for 8000 acres)
1786		Grandfather Abraham Lincoln killed by hostile Indians while planting a field of corn in the Kentucky wilderness. Tom, Lincoln's father, was a young boy and nearby when his father was killed. Tom's older brother killed the Indian.
1806		His father Thomas (he was 5'10", his son Abraham was 6'4") marries Nancy Hanks; her family is also from Virginia; his two brothers and sister were already married.
1807		Older sister Sarah born.
1809		Abraham is born in a one-room log cabin, February 12, near present-day Hodgenville, Kentucky.
1811	2	Family moves 10 miles away, to a 230-acre farm on Knob Creek, Kentucky.

YEAR	AGE	EVENTS
1812	3	Abraham's brother, Thomas, is born but he dies in infancy.
1816	7	Family moves to Indiana. Attends school briefly.
1817	8	After shooting a wild turkey, Abraham is overcome with remorse and never hunts again.
1818	9	After being kicked in the head by a horse, Abraham is briefly thought to be dead. His mother, Nancy Hanks Lincoln, dies, apparently of "milk sickness."
1819	10	His father marries Sarah Bush Johnston, a widow with three children (12, 8 and 5) (father called her Sally). Lincoln became very close to his new mother (still loved his "Angel Mother"). Only family book, the Bible. Favorite book, *Life of Washington*.
1820	11	Attends school briefly.
1821	12	Attends school for a few months.
1824	14	Does plowing and planting and works for hire for neighbors. Attends school in the fall and winter. Borrows books and reads whenever possible. *Robinson Crusoe, Pilgrim's Progress, Aesop's Fables*.

YEAR	AGE	EVENTS
1828	19	On January 20 his married sister, Sarah, dies in childbirth. A.L. takes flatboat to New Orleans with Allen Gentry (paid $25 for three-month trip). During trip they fight off a robbery attack by seven black men. Observes slave auction.
1830	21	Family moves 200 miles to Illinois, near Decatur, on uncleared land along the Sangamon River. Makes first political speech promoting the improvement of navigation on the Sangamon River.
1831	22	Takes flatboat to New Orleans for Denton Offutt (for $12/month). Then becomes a clerk in Offutt's New Salem, Illinois, store and sleeps in the back. Wrestles "strongest" man in the county, Jack Armstrong, to a draw [becomes good friends and years later successfully defends son, Duff, from murder charge]. Learns basic math, reads Shakespeare and Robert Burns and participates in a local debating society.

YEAR AGE EVENTS

YEAR	AGE	EVENTS
1832	23	Spends 90 days in the state militia during Black Hawk War (elected Captain, re-enlists as private after company is disbanded). Runs for state legislature, gives first campaign speech, loses (only two weeks to campaign, own precinct gives him 277-7 vote). Store he is working in goes out of business. Buys another store in New Salem with William Berry.
1833	24	After the store fails, he is badly in debt. Appointed postmaster in New Salem ($50/year), and Deputy County Surveyor.
1834	25	Elected to Illinois General Assembly for two years (as a Whig) ($3/day in session). Begins to study law. Meets Stephen A. Douglas, 21, a Democrat.
1835	26	Illinois General Assembly. Former store partner, Berry, dies, increasing Lincoln's debt to $1000. Eventually pays off debts, becomes known as "Honest Abe." Ann Rutledge dies from fever at age 22. Romantic connection was probably a myth.
1836	27	Reelected to Illinois General Assembly, by now a leader of the Whig party. Licensed to practice law. "Courts" Mary Owens, 28. Has an episode of severe depression in December.

YEAR	AGE	EVENTS
1837	28	Illinois General Assembly. Helps get state capital moved from Vandalia to Springfield. Moves to Springfield. Becomes law partner of John T. Stuart law firm (Stuart and Lincoln). Proposes marriage to Mary Owens, is turned down and courtship ends.
1838	29	Reelected to Illinois General Assembly, becomes Whig floor leader. Successfully defends Henry Truett in a famous murder case.
1839	30	Illinois General Assembly. Travels through nine counties in central and eastern Illinois as a lawyer on the 8th Judicial Circuit. Admitted to practice in United States Circuit Court. Meets Mary Todd, 21, at a dance. She is also being courted by Stephen A. Douglas.
1840	31	Reelected to Illinois General Assembly. Argues first case before Illinois Supreme Court. Becomes engaged to Mary Todd.
1841	32	Illinois General Assembly. Ends Stuart-Lincoln law partnership, forms new law partnership with Stephen T. Logan. Breaks off engagement to Mary Todd (it is a stormy relationship). Has episode of depression. Makes a steamboat trip to Kentucky and sees twelve slaves chained together.

YEAR	AGE	EVENTS
1842	33	Does not seek re-election. Resumes courtship of Mary Todd. Accepts challenge to a duel (with swords) by Democratic state auditor James Shields (insulting letters may have been written by Mary and another girl). Duel averted because Abe explains the letters, which caused the problem. Marries Mary Todd (1818–1882) on November 4 in the Edwards' (sister and brother-in-law) parlor before a few close friends. Rides off in the rain to their first home, a furnished room in the Globe Tavern for four dollars a month.
1843	34	Unsuccessful in try for the Whig nomination for U.S. House of Representatives. Son Robert Todd born (died 1926, aged 83).
1844	35	Moves into home in Springfield, bought for $1500 with financial help from Mary's father (originally one floor, ten years later added second floor) and lives there for 17 years, rest of sons born there. Ends partnership with Logan, begins partnership with William Herndon (never dissolved). Pays off the last of his New Salem debts.

YEAR	AGE	EVENTS
1846	37	Elected to U.S. House of Representatives (30th Congress). Son Edward Baker born (died 1850, 4 years old).
1847	38	Serves in U.S. House of Representatives. Lives in boarding house in Washington, DC. Wife and children are with her family in Kentucky.
1848	39	Serves in U.S. House of Representatives.
1849	40	Leaves politics to practice law (his opposition to the Mexican War was unpopular). Granted U.S. Patent No. 6,469 (only president ever granted a patent).
1850	41	Son William (Willie) Wallace born (died in 1862, 12 years old); son Edward dies. "Honest Abe" gains reputation as an outstanding lawyer (one of top lawyers in state, earns a fee of $5000 from Illinois R.R.).
1851	42	Lincoln's father dies at 73 (never met Mary or grandchildren).
1853	44	Son Thomas (Tad) born (died in 1871, 18 years old).
1854	45	Gets back into politics because of his opposition to the repeal of the Missouri Compromise. Elected to State Legislature, resigns to try for U.S. Senate.

YEAR	AGE	EVENTS
1855	46	Does not get chosen by the Illinois legislature to be U.S. Senator.
1856	47	Joins Republican party. Helps organize the new party in his state. At first Republican convention gets 110 votes for vice-presidential nomination, bringing him national attention.
1857	48	In Springfield he speaks against the Dred Scott decision.
1858	49	Wins acquittal in a murder trial of Duff Armstrong by using an almanac that reported the height of the moon in order to discredit a witness, and making an impassioned tearful plea on behalf of the mother, widow Armstrong. Nominated to be the Republican senator from Illinois opposing Democrat Stephen A. Douglas. Gives "House Divided" speech at state convention in Springfield. Debates Douglas (seven debates) before large audiences (debates eventually published). First called Douglas-Lincoln Debates because of S.D.'s fame.
1859	50	Illinois legislature chooses Douglas for the U.S. Senate over Lincoln by a vote of 54 to 46 (more votes, fewer districts).

YEAR	AGE	EVENTS
1860	51	Delivers "Right Makes Might" speech at Cooper Institute, NYC, February 27, and a speech on slavery in New Haven, Connecticut. Elected 16th president (33 states in union), VP Hannibal Hamlin. [Opponents, Northern Democrats –Stephen A. Douglas, Southern Democrats – John C. Breckinridge, Constitutional Union – John Bell.] [Receives 180 of 303 possible electoral votes and 40 percent of popular vote.] Grows beard.
1861	52	Gives brief farewell to friends and supporters in Springfield and leaves by train for Washington. Delivers first Inaugural Address. Civil War begins (7 states secede, eventually 4 more joined them for a total of 11 confederate states; 4 border states didn't secede but permitted slavery).
1862	53	Son William dies (12 years old). While A.L. is riding from The Soldiers' Home, his summer residence in Washington, a bullet passes through his top hat. Security is increased but not by much. Later, it is shot off again.
1863	54	Issues Emancipation Proclamation. First draft law passed. Proclaims first Thanksgiving Day. Delivers Gettysburg Address (Nov. 19). West Virginia becomes a state.

YEAR AGE EVENTS

YEAR	AGE	EVENTS
1864	55	Reelected president, VP Andrew Johnson. [Republican convention changes name to National Union Party for this election]. Opponent, Democrat – (former General) George B. McClellan [Lincoln gets 212 of 233 electoral votes and 55 percent of popular vote; election in doubt until Sherman takes Atlanta, "Atlanta is ours and fairly won." Soldier votes made the difference in many states.] [New York, Pennsylvania, and Ohio, very close. If he had lost these states (and a few others) McClellan could have won.]
1865	56	Gives second inaugural address, "...Malice towards none, charity for all..." following a drunken rambling talk by V.P. Johnson. Civil War ends (April 9), gives last public address from second floor of the White House (April 11). Shot by John Wilkes Booth (April 14) at Ford's Theatre, Lincoln dies in Washington (April 15). (Booth shot dead on April 26.) Lincoln buried in Springfield, Illinois (May 4). 13th Amendment passes, freeing all slaves [In 1861 Congress had passed a 13th Amendment saying slavery would never be abolished. Never ratified by states because of secession].

YEAR	AGE	EVENTS
1901		Because of fear of the body being, or having been, stolen, his tomb is opened and 20 or so people, including his only remaining son, Robert, view body to be sure it is still there. It was still recognizable. Then buried under heavy concrete and a magnificent monument.
1909		Lincoln penny, celebrating the 100th anniversary of Lincoln's birth, first minted (see Lincoln Lore #32).
1922		Lincoln Memorial dedicated in Washington, DC (see Lincoln Lore #26).
1941		Mount Rushmore National Museum, South Dakota, completed: Washington, Jefferson, T. Roosevelt, and Lincoln carved in granite.

VI

LINCOLN ON
THE WEB

The Internet offers many wonderful opportunities to learn about Lincoln. Here are a few good sites:

http://abrahamlincolnassociation.org/

> Abraham Lincoln Association – Organized in 1908 to spearhead the national celebration of the Lincoln's 100th birthday. Offers some marvelous research avenues and resources, including "The Lincoln Log," which can tell you what Lincoln was doing on any given day of his life.

https://digital.lib.niu.edu/illinois/lincoln

> Abraham Lincoln Historical Digitization Project – Lincoln/Net presents historical materials from Abraham Lincoln's Illinois years (1830–1861), including Lincoln's writings and speeches, as well as other materials illuminating antebellum Illinois.

https://lincoln-institute.org/

> Abraham Lincoln Institute (The Life and Legacy of President Lincoln) – Includes symposia archives, book award winners, primary source collections, and more.

http://www.abrahamlincolnonline.org/lincoln.html

> Abraham Lincoln Online.org – offers Lincoln news, discussion, Lincoln speeches, historic places connected to Lincoln, Lincoln events, Lincoln books, Lincoln resources, and Lincoln links.

https://www.alplm.org/

> Abraham Lincoln Presidential Library and Museum – Official website of the Abraham Lincoln Presidential Library and Museum.

https://rogerjnorton.com/Lincoln2.html

> Abraham Lincoln Research Site – A biography, photographs, and lots of information about Abraham Lincoln.

https://www.loc.gov/

> Library of Congress – The Library of Congress has placed a number of their Lincoln holdings online including prints and documents. See also the next listing.

https://www.loc.gov/collections/abraham-lincoln-papers/about-this-collection/

> Mr. Lincoln's Virtual Library – Maintained by the Library of Congress. This website includes a gallery of Lincoln manuscripts from the Robert Todd Lincoln and Alfred Whital Stern collections of the Library of Congress.

http://www.historyplace.com/lincoln/index.html

> The History Place Presents Abraham Lincoln – timeline of Lincoln's life.

EPILOGUE

I have gotten to know Abraham Lincoln very well over the last few decades. He has become more that a role model; he has become a friend. I am in awe of many aspects of his character, including his ability to continually grow and learn. The most remarkable attribute of Lincoln, in my opinion, is how he could combine a driving ambition and self-confidence with so little ego and so much humility. It is almost paradoxical. Once he developed a vision of what he wanted, or felt needed to be done, he seemed impervious to the petty feelings which plague most of the rest of us.

An example took place in 1861 when Secretary of State Seward and Lincoln made a late house call on General McClellan, the recently appointed general in chief of the Union Army. Rather than see them, McClellan retired to his bedroom. Seward and others were outraged. Lincoln merely said, "All I want out of General McClellan is a victory, and if to hold his horse will bring it, I will hold his horse."

McClellan didn't end up winning battles, or even fighting often enough to satisfy Lincoln, and so he fired him – twice actually. But it was for performance, and not for petty grievances.

Lincoln was an adult, in the finest sense of that word.

There are a few aspects of Lincoln's life that continue to perplex me as a father and grandfather. I have tried to get a better understanding of his relationship with his father and his eldest son, Robert. Most of his personal relationships, even the one with his complicated and often difficult wife, seem to be able to be studied and understood. But his relationships with his father and Robert still make me wonder.

We know Lincoln didn't want to become his father. Some scholars say that served as the driving force in Lincoln's personal development. We know that he considered himself his father's "indentured servant" (which in effect he was) until he reached the age of 21. He not only helped on his own farm, he was loaned out and worked for others, all earnings going to the father. Thus, Lincoln was able to spend less than a year in a classroom in his entire life. While Lincoln's mother, and then his stepmother, encouraged his reading and self-education, his father felt it interfered with his work, which of course it did.

What I find amazing is that once Lincoln was on his own, and marrying and having children and living within 100 miles of his father, Lincoln's father never met Mary Lincoln or any of their four children (one of whom was even named after him). Lincoln married in 1842; Lincoln's father died in 1851. Lincoln did not attend the funeral. Lincoln had sent his father some money to help buy a larger farm. After Lincoln was elected president, but before he left for Washington, he did visit his deceased father's farm and spent time with his stepmother.

Robert's relationship with his father is a little easier to understand. There is no doubt there was great love between them, but rapport was another matter. When "Bob" was growing up his father was just beginning his professional and political career. For more than half of any year Lincoln would be away from home, either on the legal circuit or on political business. Young Lincoln became much closer to his mother than his father, and was never "spoiled" as were his younger brothers, who shared time with their father not only in his law office but in the White House. During the presidency Robert was away, first at prep school in New Hampshire, and then at Harvard. After delivering the Cooper Union speech in New York City in 1860, candidate Lincoln did visit Robert at his school in Exeter, New Hampshire. There are conflicting accounts of how much time they spent together during Lincoln's presidency. Apparently his son did write one letter to his father requesting a postmaster position for someone who had approached him at college. The president reportedly wrote Robert and directed him to concentrate on his studies saying if there were any more such petitions he would be taken out of school. Robert is said to have carried that letter from then on to use whenever a request was made of him.

One of Lincoln's secretaries, John Hay, was the same age as Robert and they became good friends. Because Hay actually lived at the White House when Robert was at school, and worked closely with Lincoln every day, perhaps he became the son Robert couldn't be.

Robert was not with his father when he was shot at the Ford Theater, but was with him when he died the next morning. Robert went on to great business and professional success and acclaim. But he never seemed completely comfortable being the living representative of his father and grew more reticent about talking about President Lincoln as he grew older. While Robert fully expected to be buried in Springfield, Illinois, with his father, mother, and brothers, his wife didn't want him to be in his father's shadow any longer and arranged for him to be buried in Arlington National Cemetery.

My personal study of Lincoln will continue to try and help me better understand his father and son relationships.

INDEX

AUTHOR BIO

Dr. Fred Antil, often dressed as our 16th president, has been sharing stories about Lincoln for almost 30 years. It started in his grandchildren's "read to the children" program. After a few visits to the schools he decided to dress up as Lincoln – the students loved it. Then, after getting requests from adult audiences, he began a rigorous study of Lincoln.

He has an extensive Lincoln library, has visited every place Lincoln has lived or spent much time, and every major Civil War battlefield.He has given hundreds of presentations, and loves surprising even the most dedicated Lincoln buff with lesser-known facts/stories.

Fred's career was spent in organizational and human resource development, both in business and academia. He holds degrees from Cornell (BS), George Washington (MS), and Columbia (MA, EdD) Universities. He served as an officer in the U.S. Marine Corps, and lives in Warminster, Pennsylvania.

The History Club

Happy Birthday Mr. Lincoln

Two days before our next meeting will be Abraham Lincoln's 209th birthday. It seems appropriate we examine his life and his contribution to the America we know today. While Lincoln has deservedly achieved iconic status, he was very human and we will learn about the man, not the myth.

Join us, and bring a friend.

Wednesday, February 14th
10:00 a.m.
KC Music Room

There may be a surprise guest as we meet "Honest Abe," "The Rail- Splitter," "The Great Emancipator," "Father Abraham," our 16th President, and just plain Abraham Lincoln Esq.

Questions may be directed to Fred Antil @ 607-592-0753 or fha1@cornell.edu.

Join us for a Special ACE Advantage Presidents Day Presentation

One Man's Search for Abraham Lincoln

Date: February 13, 2018

Time: 1·00pm

Location: HighPoint Law Offices Classroom

This event is open to all ACE Advantage Clients and their Friends and Family. Admission is free, but reservations are required. **215-997-9773**

How much do you know about this beloved president? Did you ever want to meet him in person? If so, then please join us on **February 13 at 1:00pm** for a very special presentation by fellow ACE Client Mr Frederick H Antil Mr Antil is very much in demand for his depiction of President Lincoln and has performed as Lincoln all over the country He is a published author, retired Ivy League College professor as well as an officer in the U.S. Marine Corps. As a historian, Mr Antil has devoted years to his research of Lincoln and the Civil War and is coming to share his insights with you

To register for this special ACE Event please call the office **215-997-9773** or go to the website and check out the calendar of events. Refreshments will be served!

200 Highpoint Drive # 211 Chalfont, PA 18914

www.highpointlawoffices.com

An Evening With

Abe Lincoln

Abe Lincoln is coming to Newfield on tour. Abe will be discussing Newfield and national issues with a local politician. Abe will deliver some of his speeches. The public is encouraged to ask Mr. Lincoln questions.

There will be a display of CIVIL WAR ARTIFACTS by Danny Wheeler, Commander
Sons of the Union Veterans

Abe Lincoln: Mr. Fred Antil

Local Legislator: Mr. Daniel Winch

Date: **Friday, February 16, 2001**
Time: **7:00 P. M.**
Location: **Newfield High School Auditorium**

Sponsor: Newfield Republican Committee

Lincoln on the Civil War

Free reading and discussion Program for Adults
at the Southworth Library
with Dr. Fred Antil

Introductory Meeting:

Thursday, September 6 at 7 p.m.

Join the conversation!

This free program will explore the issues of freedom, civic duty, slavery and the Constitution through Lincoln's speeches with Fred Antil, local Lincoln Historian. For more information about the series & to register, please contact Diane Pamel at 607-844-4782 during library open hours or at southworth@twcny.rr.com.

Program Dates:
- October 4
- October 18
- November 1
- November 15
- 7 - 8:30 p.m.

"We are excited to celebrate our local connection with Abraham Lincoln and the impact he continues to have on our nation as we examine these speeches," says Diane Pamel, Library Director. The Southworth Library Lincoln Center Addition, opened in June 2011, was funded in part through the sale of an original copy of the speech given by President Lincoln after his re-election in 1864 that had been bequeathed to the library. Join us as we explore his legacy.

This program is sponsored by the New York Council for the Humanities